"Phil Callaway has done it again! This Dave Barry of Christian humor offers the perfect blend between mirth and message. As one who loves to laugh, I've been a fan of Phil's writing for years. And this book about slowing down and enjoying life is full of hearty laughs, honest reflection, and sound spiritual advice. So don't just stand there reading this book jacket. Buy a copy, walk to the park, and start reading it. You won't regret the peace and quiet, you won't regret the walk, and you certainly won't regret the laughter."

—Martha Bolton,
Bob Hope staff writer and author of *Didn't My Skin Used to Fit?*

"The best teachers remind us more than they instruct us, drawing us back in endearing ways to truths we have neglected to our own misery. This book does exactly that. As an added bonus you will love Phil's trademark humor—a reminder that those who laugh not only last longer—they learn better."

—Joel Freeman
NBA chaplain and author of *God Is Not Fair*

"Phil's storytelling has never been better than this. He doesn't just have his finger on the pulse of today's families, he has a stethoscope."

—Mike Yorkey,
coauthor of *Every Man's Battle* and former editor of *Focus on the Family*

"Anyone who can quote A.W. Tozer and the Eagles in the same book is okay with me! Phil has done it again. He's taken me into his life and made me laugh at myself. How does he do it? By capturing the yearning of a heart hungry for God. We're all struggling to make the Christian life a reality instead of a play, and every page of this book brings us one step closer."

—Chris Fabry,
broadcaster and author of *At the Corner of Mundane and Grace*

"Reading Phil Callaway is like panning for gold, but with this noticeable difference: *every* pan reveals a genuine nugget of glittering humor—so clever, so apt, so outrageous that you will bless God for having given us the ability to laugh. In this book, Phil takes on our hurry-up existence—the rush, the crush that closes in on so many in our materialist, consumerist society. As time gets squeezed, how do we rediscover the traditional values and habits that made life so wonderful in yesteryear? These pages will help you find the answer!"

—Paul L. Maier,
professor and author of *Pontius Pilate* and *Flames of Rome*

WHO PUT MY LIFE ON *FAST-FORWARD?*

PHIL CALLAWAY

HARVEST HOUSE PUBLISHERS
Eugene, Oregon 97402

Cover by Left Coast Design, Portland, Oregon

Illustrations by Mary Chambers

WHO PUT MY LIFE ON FAST-FORWARD?

Copyright © 2002 by Phil Callaway
Published by Harvest House Publishers
Eugene, Oregon 97402

Library of Congress Cataloging-in-Publication Data

Callaway, Phil, 1961-
    Who put my life on fast-forward? / Phil Callaway.
      p. cm.
    ISBN 0-7369-0776-9
      1. Simplicity—Religious Aspects—Christianity. 2. Christian life. 3. Callaway, Phil,
1961—-Anecdotes. I. Title

    BV4647.S48 C35 2002
    241'.4—dc21   2001039849

Printed in the United States of America.

03 04 05 06 07 08 09 10 11 / BP-MS / 10 9 8 7 6 5 4 3

*In memory of Cordell Darling,
who lived this book, impacted a community,
and helped me balance my world.*

Contents

A Note from the Author

It's rather nice writing a book on slowing down. When your editor calls to find out how you're doing with the deadline, you merely tell him, "I'm practicing what I preach. I'm hanging out in my hammock, sipping iced tea." He has little recourse but to talk about the weather.

This book was two years in the writing and many more in the convincing. Allow me to explain. My world is oftentimes on fast-forward and I can't seem to locate the stop button on the remote control. Deadlines come quickly. Appointments come often. Like you, I struggle to balance a busy life, and sometimes I fail.

Readers don't want to hear from someone who has failed, do they?

My editors Terry Glaspey and Carolyn McCready felt they did. When you're about to be operated on, you're not looking for a doctor who has never felt pain, they insisted. Furthermore, because of my experiences of the past few years, they both felt I was the one to write such a book.

First a word about what this book is not.

It is not a longing for simpler or better times. It is not *Johnny Appleseed* meets *Martha Stewart Living*. Don't get me wrong, I loved the good old days when rental car agencies took cash and getting across the ocean took weeks, but I do not live there. In Ecclesiastes, the teacher writes, "Do not say, 'Why were the old days better than these?' For it is not wise to ask such questions." We cannot turn the clock back, but we can wind it up and set it right.

When the *London Times* wanted to produce a story on a decaying culture, the editors summoned the brightest authors of the day to respond to the question, "What's Wrong with the World?" Most of the responses were deep and lengthy and eloquent. But the most insightful was the simplest. It came from one of my favorite thinkers, G.K. Chesterton, who, with a wry smile on his face I'm sure, wrote this response:

> Dear Sirs:
>
> I am.
>
> Sincerely yours,
> G.K. Chesterton

In the same way, I must admit that I am to blame. I have put my world on fast-forward. No, I did not invent the split-screen television, the omnipresent cell phone, or the temperature-controlled doghouse, but I am responsible for the speeded-up life I have lived. Such an outlook gives me hope that things can be bettered and balanced and changed.

It is my hope that the stories and practical remedies proposed in this book will bring about the same change in you that they have in me.

Special thanks belong to so many. Allow me to name just a few: My wife Ramona is the very best thing about me. My finest critic and closest friend, she practices what I preach. Our children—Jeffrey, Stephen, and Rachael—have brightened our home with their mischief, scratched some blackboards with their fingernails, and softened our hearts with their love. Applause also belongs to my friend Mary Chambers (one of the best cartoonists to ever live in Alba, Missouri—population 27), who could have laughed at my ideas, but instead brought them to life. Mary models the message of this book and has seven children, thus providing ample proof that there's hope for you, me, and anyone else who is frantically searching for the stop button on the remote control.

Phil Callaway
Alberta, Canada

1000 Miles an Hour

Man is flying too fast for a world that is round.
Soon he will catch up with himself in a great rear-
end collision, and man will never know
that what hit him from behind was man.

—James Thurber

On my desk is a book on stress. The first 31 pages consist of something the authors call The Stress Test. Picking up a pencil just moments ago, I began answering questions such as "If you could change your life in one major way, what would that be?"

I paused briefly to consider the question, then wrote, "I would quit taking this test."

After all, I couldn't concentrate. My mind was dizzy with all I had to do. I was staring down the barrel of a dozen deadlines. My daughter's temperature had reached 102 degrees. Bills were threatening. The phone was ringing. And the lengthy form reminded me that my taxes were due in a week.

Writers of stress tests should take into consideration that the person filling them out is probably in no mood to answer questions such as "On a scale of one to ten, how frustrated do you feel right now?" So rather than hit you over the head with another comprehensive survey, here is my New Condensed Stress Test. You won't even need a pencil.

Are you living in the twenty-first century?
Are you reading this book?

If you answered yes to either of these questions, chances are that your world is on fast-forward and you are wondering where to get off.

Scientists say the earth is spinning at just over 1000 miles an hour and that we're racing around the sun at 67 times that speed. To make matters worse, our solar system is moving within our galaxy at 600,000 miles an hour. If it weren't for a little apple that hit Sir Isaac Newton on the head, we would be hurled into space at an early age (something that would certainly increase our insurance premiums).

Lately we seem to be picking up even more speed.

Pollsters say that 86 percent of Americans claim to be chronically stressed out. The *New England Journal of Medicine* reported that 44 percent of American adults had one or more substantial symptoms of stress following the terrorist attacks on September 11, 2001, and nine out of ten had stress reactions to some degree. The National Center for Health Statistics reports that almost 1 million people a year lose their lives to diseases caused by unmanaged stress. To cope we now ingest 60,000 pounds of aspirins, tranquilizers, and sleeping pills a day. Thankfully, that's not per person, but the sum is still staggering.

We change jobs between seven to ten times in our lifetime. According to *U.S. News & World Report,* women, on average, do so every 5.8 years and men every 7.6 years. We change houses even more rapidly. Back in 1835 Alexis de Tocqueville wrote, "A man builds a house in which to spend his old age, and he sells it before the roof is on." *Atlantic Monthly* reports that the average American occupies 12 or 13 residences in a lifetime, twice as many as the average person in Britain or France and four times as many as the typical

Irish. My aging mother informs me that since marrying my father (centuries ago), they have lived in 32 different houses.

Our children change schools and friends about as often as they change their socks, while we parents change churches, neighbors, dentists, and grocery stores. For many of us, busyness, fatigue, and stress have become unwelcome companions on this journey.

One medical doctor said, "I am dying of easy accessibility. If Alexander Graham Bell walked into my office, I'd punch him in the nose. If he called, you can be sure I'd put him on hold." So many people now answer their cell phones in the middle of the night, inadvertently jamming the antenna into their ears, that doctors have given the syndrome a name: yuppie ear. I kid you not. "Beepilepsy" is the momentary panic suffered when one's pager goes off. How times have changed since Daniel Boone said, "All you need for happiness is a good gun, a good horse, and a good wife" (I'm not sure if it was in that particular order or not).

More than 30 years ago, about the time Bob Dylan was singing "The times, they are a changin'," Alvin Toffler's *Future Shock* sold millions, warning of a

> roaring current of change, a current so powerful today that it overturns institutions, shifts our values and shrivels our roots. Change is the process by which the future invades our lives... unless man quickly learns to control the rate of change in his personal affairs as well as in society at large, we are doomed to a massive adaptational breakdown.

The same year Toffler's book was released, on a scorching hot July day, my mom and dad buckled four kids into a 1965 Pontiac Parisienne, complete with magnetic vinyl seat covers, and pointed it toward Toronto, Ontario, Canada. (I also smuggled two sparrows aboard in a cornflakes box.) My father was an ordained minister and I think the closest I ever saw him come to swearing was when our air conditioner blew a gasket. But for a ten-year-old boy, the world looked pretty good from that backseat. Birds sang sweetly right there in the car (much to my parents' amazement), and we were already too far from home to warrant their return. I sipped my first root beer that day, ice cold from a gas station icebox. My sister Ruth taught me to play Roshambo (Rock-Paper-Scissors) and I beat her badly. Six days, three flat tires, and 2300 miles later we arrived at our destination, tired but happy. I had mourned the flight of my two birds on that trip, honed the art of playing an imaginary drum set, and learned to shoot at frogs with a BB gun (thankfully I never hit one).

Last week I made the same journey at 600 miles an hour in less than four hours. As I hurried through the airport to catch a shuttle bus, I remembered that trip 30 Julys ago, and wondered if our world is really any better off.

I'm not the only one wondering.

When I told a friend in the office next to mine about this book project, she laughed and said, "Hurry up and write it. I need it today!" Then she planted her elbows on her desk, let out a soft sigh and said, "What can we do to balance things...to slow our lives down?"

That is one of the questions I hope to answer in the next few hundred pages. I will not do this with thousands of statistics you have already read—more data to tire you out. You already know that we are running at an unprecedented pace. That change easily engenders fear, worry, and aspirin-sized headaches. Instead, I will tell my own story (though I wish some of it weren't true) and the stories of others who have discovered humorous and creative ways of climbing off the merry-go-round without spraining their ankles.

During the past few years I have talked with hundreds of people about their pace of life, asking them what has helped them most. From the resulting mountain of material I've uncovered six secrets I can't wait to share with you. Some of the advice comes from billionaires, millionaires, CEOs, and VIPs, but mostly it comes from regular folk like you and me, people who are so tired they can barely lace up their Velcro tennis shoes. It is my hope that you'll discover as they have that peace, simplicity, and joy are achievable—even on a planet that spins at 1000 miles an hour.

PART ONE
Even Ants Have Time to Attend Picnics

*To be unavailable to friends and family, to be unable
to find time for the sunset, to whiz through our
obligations without time for a single, mindful breath,
this has become the model of a successful life.*

—WAYNE MULLER

There is more to life than merely increasing its speed.

—GANDHI

1

Going Underground

We must show a new generation of nervous,
almost frantic [people] that...speed and noise
are evidences of weakness, not strength.
—A.W. TOZER (1897-1963)

On August 13, 1971 (a Friday, I believe), the devil invited millions of demons from the far corners of the Western Hemisphere to the annual Creative Chaos Convention held 300 miles beneath Texas. It was a hot day even above ground, and attendance was mandatory.

"Fellow enemies," Satan began in his keynote address, "we have had some victories. We have split some churches and burned some Bibles, and we've got them arguing about music again like we did in the 1600s. I congratulate you on a terrible job!"

The demons began lobbing fiery darts at one another and booing loudly. Lifting his hand, Satan calmed their gleeful enthusiasm. "But let's be honest—though none of us finds it easy," he continued. "We haven't stopped these Christians from reading their Bibles, loving their neighbors, or worshiping God. It's time we tried something else."

"Like what?" shouted a particularly ugly little demon whose name tag read "Hal."

Satan emitted a long and sinister cackle, then adjusted his notes and gazed out over the darkened auditorium. "We will gradually distract them," he wheezed. "We will keep them from God by making them too busy with other things. Oh, let them go to church, but start stealing their time. If they have no time for a relationship with Jesus, we've got 'em."

"But how?" shouted ugly little Hal, who was still trembling at the mention of That Name. "How do we steal their time?"

"Redefine success for them. It's not about people or faithfulness anymore, it's about things. Make them equate success with stuff. Keep them borrowing, borrowing, borrowing. Lower the prime rate. Replace the front porch with a garage. Convince them that they need bigger houses and more cars. Keep the husbands and wives working longer hours to get out of debt and rarely let them see their kids. I've hated the family since the beginning. This just might fix it."

"Is that all?" shouted another demon near the back.

"No, I'm just getting started," said Satan, who was met with another enthusiastic round of jeers and catcalls.

"Make them comfortable and complacent. Blind them to the needs of others. And would someone invent seedless watermelons? They're having way too much fun spitting them. I hate it when Christians laugh."

"What else, what else?" sneered Hal, just before being pelted by a rotten egg.

"Make silence a fearful thing. Create so much noise that they can't hear the still, small voice of God. Turn the music up in restaurants and supermarkets, pound their minds with 24-hour news channels, invent something better than that awful 8-track and keep the music loud. The sound systems in our cars are lousy—do something about that. There isn't nearly enough junk mail either, so have it increased. And we need more television channels. How about a shopping channel? See if you can get away with a golf channel, though I doubt you can. Offer free products and sweepstakes and trips and pyramid marketing schemes. Get them to take excessive vacations and return broke. Keep them away from nature. Let them find their rest in amusement parks, sporting events, and movies, and could someone increase the cussing in Hollywood? There isn't nearly enough cussing. Hal, you take care of that."

You could barely hear Satan now above the rising enthusiasm. But he wasn't finished.

"Speed up the world!" he yelled above the roar of the minions. "Don't give those Christians time to think. Or rest. Make them too tired to walk with God. Too weary to lift a hand to help others. Keep them busy with good things—with programs and charts and reports—but don't let them rely on Christ. Let them think they can get by on their own. Let them sacrifice their health and their family and their God on the altar of busyness. Then they will be ours."

Over Satan's sinister cackle, the demons began to stomp and chant, "We will, we will, rock them."

Some say the standing ovation is still going on.

2

Blindfolded

Don't leave your office to go get a drink
without a slip of paper in your hand. Without the
paper it looks like you have nothing to do.
—ADVICE IN AN OFFICE MEMO

I walked the halls of my old high school the other day. Ghosts were everywhere, alongside memories of classmates and teachers and trips to the principal's office. One teacher in particular liked to send me there. He was a short, wiry man who knew me only by birth date. "Hi, July 26," he'd say, passing me in the hall. He loved to spend social studies class warning of conspiracies and dictatorships and the end of the world.

During my senior year of high school, he announced plans to retire. "What will you do?" I asked him one day after he was through lecturing us on how dark the times were. "I've just bought a cabin in the mountains and I'm stocking it with canned goods," he replied. His family would bow out of the rat race, step back in time, slow down. "It's the devil's conspiracy, you know," he said.

I remember laughing at the time, even pitying him. But a few years ago the cabin started beckoning me as well. A recurring nightmare did not help. In my nightmare it is early morning. My foot is heavy on the gas pedal of our '95 Ford

Windstar as I speed down the interstate. The windshield is cracked, rust is creeping through the paint on the hood, but I can see neither.

I am driving blindfolded.

The honking of horns and the jarring of speed bumps alert me to the danger, and I clutch at the blindfold, ripping it from my face. It is too late. I am airborne now, launched from the edge of a cliff. On impulse I hit the brakes. It is futile. Like Wile E. Coyote, I am hurtling through space, with no air brakes and no animator to save me.

Waking, I stare at a stucco ceiling, sweating on a cold winter's night.

The nightmare began arriving with greater frequency a few years ago. Events had combined to push me past the point of no return. I was driving too fast along life's interstate, unable to locate the compass points, incapable of finding rest stops along the way. Somewhere on an Alaska highway a sign warns: "Choose your rut carefully. You'll be in it for the next 200 miles." But so many of us miss the warning signs. Blindfolded by our quest for success, we are driving in a major rut. We are missing the quiet reflection that gives birth to wisdom. The laughter born of deep friendships. The joy of simplicity.

Letters cross my desk every day in response to my book *Making Life Rich Without Any Money*. One, from a millionaire in Chicago, states simply, "If I would have practiced your methods for simple living in a complex world ten years ago, I'd still have my family." Another asks, "Do you really believe that the best things in life can't be bought? If that's true, I have wasted the last 30 years of my life." For those three decades, this financial investor had bought into the Cult of More (.COM). Its creed is simple: More money brings more prestige and freedom, which equals more recognition, more influence, more satisfaction, more love, more security, and in the end, more peace.

All one needs for membership in the Cult of More is a thick blindfold.

I recently spoke to an audience of a few thousand men. I started with one simple question: "In the last 24 hours, how many of you have told someone, 'I'm tired'?" Their response made me wonder if I had just asked how many wanted an ocean view condo and a yacht. Hands thrust skyward. Some men raised both of them. And they weren't just the Pentecostals!

To be busy is to be important, we reason. After all, isn't busyness the mark of a successful life? And conversely, isn't having enough time to spend a guilt-free evening on the front porch a sign of laziness?

A few years ago, when the nightmare began, I believed so. Having grown up below the poverty line, I was determined to give my children the things I had lived without. A rust-free car, a worry-free journey into financial security. Running hard to get ahead, I prided myself on being the first one to unlock the office each morning and often the last one to lock it on the way home. Weekends spelled work, evenings meant the same. And it seemed to be working. A second bestseller was in the works. The speaking circuit was a growing possibility.

One August night, as I sat aboard a jet pointed toward Ottawa, Canada, I looked over my notes for the next day's speech. Putting them aside to sip some soda, I watched the sun sink into the purple mountains to my left. An unwelcome fatigue swept over me. Closing my eyes, I pushed my seat back, unaware that an event was waiting to change my pace forever.

3

Sleepless in Ottawa

By working faithfully eight hours a day,
you may get to be a boss and
work twelve hours a day.
—ROBERT FROST

This book was born of two events. The first was a weekend writers' conference in Edmonton, Alberta, Canada, where I found myself surrounded by fellow writers who were gracious enough to listen to my stories and even laugh on cue. I talked not only of the joys of publishing, but also of some of the struggles that accompany success. Of deadlines and talk shows and balancing the demands of a rigorous schedule. Of the irony of receiving five calls a day from people wanting you to leave home and tell them how to spend quality time with their family. Were it not for a redefinition of success, a chain of accountability, and a personal mission statement, I told them, my life would be chaotic.

When I sat down, Dr. Maxine Hancock, one of Canada's most gifted orators, stood and talked candidly of her own battle to harmonize the demands of success. "One weekend my husband, Cam, and I held a marriage retreat," Maxine told us, "and it went so well that afterward, in the parking lot, the president of the sponsoring organization asked us to make this an annual event." Without a second thought, Cam responded, "Sorry, we can't. We're booked up for eight years." Maxine's mouth dropped open and by the time they reached the car, she was steaming. With a simple sentence her husband had seemingly destroyed a fabulous opportunity, to say nothing of substantial book sales. "How...how could you?" Maxine stammered, opening the car door.

"We *are* booked up," Cam told her. "We've got a family to raise and a farm to care for."

"He was absolutely right and very wise," recalled Maxine. "But I didn't appreciate his wisdom at the time."

Next on the evening's schedule was an interview with Janette Oke. Janette is Canada's most successful author, and her book sales have surpassed 20 million copies, earning her a voice around the world. But while spending the evening at Janette's table, I was struck by her down-home simplicity, her open smile, and her easy laugh. During the interview, she shied away from accolades and centered on the simple things. Though she writes three books a year, she preferred to talk about her grandchildren or her relationship with God. Hardly what you'd expect when you read a publisher's bio written about her career.

Later, Maxine, Janette, and I stood together discussing the speeded-up lives we have been asked to live. Though we weren't complaining, it struck me that each of us, in his or her own way, seemed to speak easily of busyness and stress, much like women discussing the pains of childbirth.

"You should write a book called *Who Flipped the World to Fast-Forward?*" joked Janette. I laughed. But on the drive home, the idea began to take shape. Turning off the radio, I pondered another event that made me wonder if I was as qualified as anyone to write on the subject.

※

I am pacing back and forth before an open hotel window in Ottawa, Canada's capital city. Parliament buildings tower above the picturesque Rideau Canal as sharp reminders that careers are made here—and sometimes ended. I am staying in a corner suite, greeted by an overflowing basket of fruit, chocolate, and welcome cards. Past thick drapes, yachts rock gently from side to side on the canal, like the wooden boats I carved as a kid. Cyclists pedal by, going somewhere fast. Beyond the canal, the Parliament buildings rise into the night sky. An enormous clock on the Peace Tower chimes nine times. But there is no peace tonight. Not for me.

This last year my life has been flipped upside-down. My schedule is out of control—my days long, my nights short. My standard greeting is "I am *so* busy." I wear my exhaustion like a badge of honor, the trophy of a productive life. The Chinese pictograph for "busy" is composed of two characters: heart and killing. How appropriate. The long days and short nights have taken their toll. Whenever a weekend arrives I am exhausted and often physically sick. Illness has become my Sabbath.

To make matters worse, tomorrow marks an event that has terrified me for weeks. I am to address a large hall filled with booksellers. I will tell them of my latest book and why it is important that their customers have it. The date on my schedule has been circled for months, and it has so frightened me that I have been unable to sleep for two days. Few things in life scare me more than addressing a group. In a cover story "What Scares You," *Time* magazine lists hundreds of phobias, including dentophobia (fear of dentists), phalacrophobia (fear of growing bald), and arachibutyrophobia (fear of peanut butter sticking to the roof of your mouth). I have experienced the first two, but the number one fear out there, according to the experts, is glossophobia—fear of speaking in public. I can relate. On those days I would rather wear pajamas stuffed with fiberglass insulation than speak publicly.

There in an Ottawa hotel room, my mind comes to a grinding halt. Then it flashes on the long days and short nights of pursuing success. On a wife whose health problems have left doctors mystified. On a brush with death that had left me pondering my own mortality: Back in college I had lain for several days in a hospital bed, nursing a temperature of 105 degrees. One night I awoke and overheard soft voices in the hallway. Three shadows moved slowly on the wall beside me as a doctor warned my parents, "He has a heart murmur that can be quite common, but in this case it seems to indicate a valve problem. You believe in God. Now's a good time to pray. If he gets through this, he'll have to learn to pace himself."

But the warning has gone unheeded. That is, until this night in a strange hotel room when I literally collapse on the floor, as if a cold hand has grabbed me from behind, threatening to squeeze my breath away. My mind swirls with a thousand fears, and the open window beckons. I don't know what a panic attack is, but this is as close as I'd like to come.

Earlier this same year, Neil Rudenstine, a zealous perfectionist and the president of Harvard, oversleeps one morning. He is in the midst of a million-dollar-a-day fundraising campaign at the time, so when he awakes and looks at the clock, he jumps from the bed in panic. After years of nonstop toil in a world that rewards frantic overwork and busyness, Rudenstine literally collapses. "I was exhausted," he would later tell reporters. For three months he strolled a Caribbean beach with his wife, read Lewis Thomas, and listened to Ravel before returning to his job. This week his picture is on the cover of *Newsweek* beside the bold headline—"Exhausted!"

The word sums up my situation well. I literally pull myself on hands and knees to the phone and call my wife. She prays with me, then repeats words of comfort from the Bible several times over: "My presence shall go with you, and I will give you rest."

I sleep for two hours that night and the next evening sleepwalk my way through the booksellers' event, my mind numb. Upon arriving home, one of my first stops is the doctor's office. "Phil," says the doctor, "you need three months off."

I smile. "I have bills to pay," I tell him. Though I could read Lewis Thomas or listen to Ravel, it is financially impossible for me to stroll a Caribbean beach with my wife.

It will take much more. It will take a complete rethinking of my approach to life, work, relationships, and success.

That night my wife and I walk through a wheat field near our home, suggesting changes, talking of the future, and speaking of the things that really matter. The sunlight is fading, and a glorious rainbow arches in the sky. I think of all the rainbows and sunsets I've missed, how the beauty has been a blur, not a blessing. I am weak but strangely filled with hope. Another chance is mine. I know I can never go back.

4

Remember the Sabbath?
Me Neither!

*Jesus spoke about [helping the ox out of the]
ditch on the Sabbath. But if your ox gets in
the ditch every Sabbath, you should either
get rid of the ox or fill up the ditch.*
—BILLY GRAHAM

When I was growing up, the single most miserable day of the week was without a doubt Sunday. For one thing, Sunday spelled church, which I did not fully appreciate at the time. In fact, I used to climb a tall poplar tree about nine o'clock each Sunday morning and hide behind the leaves, much like Adam and Eve, hoping my parents would forget they had a fifth child and would drive off—leaving me alone with the refrigerator.

They never did.

I loved Sunday dinner, the fatted meatloaf with assorted vegetation. The conversation. The laughter. For that one hour, there was Sabbath joy. But then came Sunday afternoon—the longest five hours of the week. Jewish texts prohibit 39 specific acts during Sabbath. My parents' list was longer. We were not allowed to throw a baseball, toss a Frisbee, yell loudly, read comic books, run in the yard, ride horses, or chew tobacco. Acceptable activities included praying, napping, reading Danny Orlis books, listening to

Billy Graham's *Hour of Decision,* and singing hymns to elderly people at the Golden Hills Lodge. When you are a boy of ten or eleven, your world does not revolve around these things.

And so I found myself in that poplar tree often on Sunday afternoon, squatting quietly, my chin in my hands. From there, I could envy the Silvers, who lived on the other side of our garden.

Mr. Silver and his son Mark spent the afternoon in their backyard throwing a football or chipping golf balls at each other. Sometimes they laughed loudly, and when the sun reached its apex they even took off their shirts. I was sure they were ripe for judgment for any one of these sins, and I watched expectantly, waiting for the ground to open up and swallow them whole. Sunday evenings were set aside for church, but I'm pretty sure the Silvers watched Walt Disney instead.

Though my parents wisely relaxed their rules over the years, to me, rest had become synonymous with boredom. And I was not the first to feel this way.

The early Christians began meeting on Sunday to commemorate the day of Jesus' resurrection. In A.D. 321, the newly converted emperor, Constantine, decreed that Sunday would be a day of rest throughout the entire Roman Empire, ushering in a period of governmentally enforced Sabbath-keeping, mandatory church attendance, and the bringing of little bags of Cheerios to church. In the sixteenth century, when religious reform swept across Europe, lengthy worship services became the norm. Their purpose was to direct thoughts heavenward and steer the faithful away from sensual temptations such as jousting or building moats.

When I was first married, I suppose I overreacted to the strict legalism of the church and began to do things my own way. Whenever possible I slept in on Sunday morning, thus avoiding church. I even began to prefer work to a forced rest.

YOU REALLY SHOULD HAVE A STRESS TEST.
I'M SUGGESTING YOU DRIVE MY KIDS TO SOCCER FOR A WEEK.

After all, didn't Jesus warn of legalism with His words, "The Sabbath was made for man, not man for the Sabbath"? Perhaps I felt like Bill Gates, who told *Time* magazine, "Just in terms of allocation of time resources, religion is not very efficient. There's a lot more I could be doing on a Sunday morning." In hindsight, my deconstruction of a Sabbath rest was partly responsible for my own crippling burnout.

The ancient rabbis taught that on the six days of creation God created the universe, but on the seventh day He created something else—*menuha,* or tranquillity, serenity, and peace. (Others have suggested that on the eighth day God said, "Let there be problems," and there were problems. But that's another book.) If God could afford to rest in creating the universe, certainly we could stand to do a little resting ourselves. Our building and creating and planning and running leave us short of breath.

The God who created the Sabbath did not do so because He is a cranky schoolteacher who garners delight from watching His students' reluctant compliance. The fourth commandment comes from a loving Father who understands us best, who does not like to see us suffer, and who knows we need to breathe deeply.

After I spoke in a church recently, the pastor made an interesting comment. "When people laugh," he said, "they exhale as if they are ridding themselves of a burden. I heard them doing that today."

A Sabbath rest allows us to breathe. To exhale. To make room for much-needed oxygen. *Rest* clears away the *rust* of the week. When we set aside our work routine, we allow other things—friendship, music, laughter, conversation, rest, and worship—to be born in its place.

A friend of mine, who built his own house on evenings and weekends, not taking a Sabbath rest for more than a year, told me the other day, "I don't have many regrets, but that is one of them. My family suffered, and so did I."

"What are you doing differently now?" I asked him.

"Sunday is no longer about me," he said, without really thinking. "It's about God...and my family. I do things with my son more now," he added, looking into the distance. "We attend church together. I hope it's not too late."

The fourth commandment is the only one that begins with the word "remember," perhaps because it is something we have forgotten. Have you forgotten the Sabbath? It's not too late to remember.

I am thankful for parents who can laugh about my times in the poplar tree. "Were we really that strict?" they asked in disbelief the other day. I told them they were and thanked them for modeling balance later on. Like my friend, Mom and Dad still center Sunday around God and others. They are both in their late seventies now, and I believe that long life has come to them partly because they have honored the Sabbath.

They still call Sunday the holy Sabbath. I once called it only Sunday, before realizing that unless I treat it as a Sabbath, there is a danger my children will only call it the weekend.

"Remember," I once heard someone say, "when we keep the Sabbath, the Sabbath will keep us."

Pause

Survey Questions:
Over the past five years has your pace of life decreased or increased?
Decreased: 31.5%
Increased: 68.5%

Would you say you are stressed:
Never: 2%
Seldom: 6%

Most of the time: 8%
Often: 24%
Some of the time: 60%

An older man in our church offered me some wise advice: "Live where you can be near your friends and where you can notice something new out your back window every day." Here is the wise counsel of a few more friends:

> I have begun practicing something I call the Sabbath Pause. Two objects remind me of it. The first is the chime of our grandfather clock—my father's gift to me a year before he died. The second is a stoplight to and from work. Though I don't always feel like it, I am learning to let these objects remind me to pause, to take a deep breath, to give thanks to God for at least one thing.
>
> —TONY DOWNER

> My own journey toward a simpler life began with a doctor's phone call: "Anne, you have breast cancer. We want to do surgery right away." I was devastated for days. I remember looking at a calendar on the fridge and wondering how many of the days I'd already circled I would have at all. My body began to change during the treatment period and I never wondered if I was too busy; my body told me. Cancer was a gift that slowed me down, brought me face-to-face with God, and changed my pace of life.
>
> —ANNE AUGSBURGER

> For our wedding my father-in-law gave us a rather unusual gift—a brand new lawnmower and rototiller. Two weeks after our wedding day

he brought them—complete with gold ribbons—
on an old truck. After pushing them to the backyard together, my new "father" gave my husband
and me a big hug and handed us a card. Later in
the house we opened it together. The card was
beautiful and inside he had written beside a big
smiley face, "These are Christian lawn tools.
They do not work on Sunday." Ever since my husband and I have developed the habit of giving
them a Sabbath rest.

—RENE DICKSON

Dinnertime is the one hour of the day when we
try whenever possible to be together as a family.
We leave the answering machine on and the television off. We start with a salad (when my wife
remembers) and end with a dessert. We try to eat
slower. We let the children know that any topic is
permissible. The conversations we've had because
of this are absolutely priceless.

—RONALD NELSON

**...if you call the Sabbath a delight and the
LORD's holy day honorable, and if you honor it
by not going your own way and not doing as
you please or speaking idle words, then you will
find your joy in the LORD, and I will cause you
to ride on the heights of the land...**

—ISAIAH 58:13-14

5

A New Beginning

One of the symptoms of an approaching
nervous breakdown is the belief that
one's work is terribly important.
—BERTRAND RUSSELL

I know of few things more disturbing to a man than having someone misplace his remote control. Perhaps the only thing more disconcerting is misplacing it himself.

One night when our children were very small, I finally got them kissed, read to, and tucked into bed; then I sat down to watch the Toronto Blue Jays beat the stuffing out of the New York Yankees from the comfort of an easy chair. My right hand moved robotically to the bookstand beside me and fished around, coming up empty.

The remote control was nowhere to be felt.

I searched under the sofa and behind the sofa and inside the sofa. Nothing. Some spare change. A doll's head. A cinnamon bun. But no remote. Before long I found myself looking in ridiculous places. The heat vent. The dog dish. The sugar jar. Still nothing. Finally, I woke the children and brought them to the living room, like a drill sergeant.

"Kids," I barked, hoping they would somehow grasp the gravity of the situation. "I cannot find the remote control. It is missing. It is gone bye-bye." They didn't have a clue what I was talking about. In fact, one of them fell asleep as I barked, landing face first on the sofa.

I woke him up and knelt before him as he wiped sleep from his eyes. Then I pleaded once again: "The remote control is gone. Where is it?"

"I have *self*-control," said my four-year-old.

But that's not what I was looking for.

Finding a piece of paper, I drew a rectangular object and scratched little square buttons inside it. Not a bad impression of a remote, I thought. Rachael, who was two, agreed. She pointed at it and said, "Ahhhh."

My heart jumped and I leaped to my feet.

"Where?" I asked.

She pointed to the door.

"Outside," she said.

Outside we went. She in her pajamas and I in my haste. Lifting her gently, I carried her in the crook of my arm. She pointed at the grass with one arm and held my neck with the other. I searched through the long grass. Nothing. I looked at Rachael. "Where?" I asked, with increasing impatience.

"Swings," she said, in her most charming voice.

I looked beneath the swing set. Nothing.

"Sandbox," she said.

I put her down and sifted through the sandbox, finding lots of things. Disgusting things. But no remote.

"Rachael," I said with a sideways glance, "come on... where?"

"In the woods," said Rachael, pointing.

I shook my head and resisted a smile. A two-year-old will do anything to stay awake. I took the child back to bed then, determined to resume my search in the morning. "I hope it doesn't rain," I told my wife, as I lay down on the living room floor, bringing my head to rest on a small purple pillow at the foot of the easy chair. The pillow seemed unusually lumpy. I thrust a hand beneath it and, as you've already guessed, came up with the remote.

Perhaps you've had your own remote control experience. They tell me that some newfangled televisions have a search button so the remote can be located a little more easily. It's a good thing. Some of us have trouble living without it. Our breath comes in short spurts. We panic. We blame others. We search in all the wrong places for something that is easily within our reach. So it is in life. We hurry from one place to the next looking for peace, never realizing that it will not be found until we slow down and stop, until we rest. Sadly most of us will go to great lengths to find something that controls our television, but we seem to avoid that which can bring our lives under control.

I got to looking at the buttons on the remote that night, partly to see if I'd drawn them correctly on my little piece of artwork. And I noticed something. There is a fast-forward button. And some movies are better watched with it on. But for the most part the movie or the game is ruined if you leave the machine on fast-forward. It's time we notice the other buttons: Pause. Stop. Play.

Grand Rapids

A few months after my Ottawa experience, I took the family to one of the most beautiful spots on earth, Banff National Park. I remember little, but one particular moment comes to mind. My son and I are standing on the banks of the Bow River. Upstream a few hundred yards, the water is turbulent, rushing over rocks in rapids made famous by numerous Hollywood films. We are here to get away from the rushing concerns of a busy life. For three days we will do little but gaze at the mountains, sit around a campfire, hike, and talk.

"You wanna see me cut the devil's throat?" I ask my son, rolling up my pants and wading in a few steps. He seems intrigued. I launch a high one straight upwards. Reaching its apex, the smooth rock plummets downward, slicing into the water, making a hollow-sounding gurgle upon entry.

"Cool," Stephen laughs, and tries it himself.

For the better part of an hour we skip stones. The river is only 60 or 70 feet wide here, so if we throw stones fast enough, they skim the surface and reach the other shore relatively unscathed. If we throw them slowly, they bounce twice, then disappear, much to our disappointment.

As I throw a stone and watch it bounce, I realize that like the stone, I do not want to disappear. I fear slowing down because I may drown in a river of poverty, loss, or regret. So I keep moving, never stopping long enough to savor the scenery. To punch "stop" on the remote. To put it aside. To rest.

Slowing down runs contrary to everything we're taught. As a teenager in church, I can remember singing "Let me burn out for Thee, Dear Lord," and I wondered who wrote it. I am a Christian. For many years it was part of my theology that only an extremely busy Christian is a productive one. I am coming to realize that there are times when our lives will be on fast-forward, but they cannot be stuck there.

We prefer to fill the quietness with noise, and to fill our calendars with errands and things to do—anything to fill the empty space. Perhaps because we were told so many times as children that our heads were empty, we've done our best to ensure that our schedules aren't.

What a contrast is the life of Jesus. When He withdrew from the crowds, the disciples couldn't believe it. "Lepers need healing," they said, "the lame must walk, the hungry must be fed. There is much to be done." But Jesus knew the value of rest. He had created plant species that will not bear fruit in the spring if they do not lie dormant in the winter. And so, the Bible tells us, He took the time to rest.

We recently bought a puppy. This little dog is not the smartest member of its species, but you can learn things when you watch her. Sometimes in the evening she curls up on my chest when I lie down on the living room floor. I always notice something right away. Her tiny heart beats faster than I can count. It slows only when she sleeps.

I'm told that the jumping mouse's heart beats between 500 and 600 times per minute. During hibernation, however, this little heart slows to 30 beats per minute. I'm not recommending permanent hibernation, but rest.

In the shadow of the Rocky Mountains, I found a delightful God-given invitation to rest. It is virtually impossible to study rocks the size of small countries, rocks that have been there since the dawn of time, and not feel small and slightly insignificant. A towering pine beside our camper reminded me that it was here before I was, and it will remain after I'm gone.

Why all the urgency? If I cannot accomplish the next task on my list today, whose world will end?

Seven years have passed. I have not achieved a perfect balance. But I'm learning to rest. I say no more often and I make less money as a result. But I'm able to spend more time in the backyard now. Playing catch with the kids. Or chasing the dog. Or working in the garden. I take more walks. Some of them on the golf course. Most of them with my wife. I write when the ideas come, and I don't sweat when they stay away. I pray more often. Each day is incomplete without time on my knees. I've yet to have a day where I couldn't give thanks for something. I'm learning that I can't control as many things as I once thought I could, but I can surrender them all to the One who is in charge.

I feel small when I'm on my knees before a God I'm just beginning to know. It's the same God who spoke to Moses, a small but significant man. Moses was leading God's people through the desert, bone weary and worn to a frazzle. "I can't do it," he kept reminding God. And he was right. He needed God's help. "I'm just a little guy," he said. "I stagger, I stutter, I stumble." And God comforted him with the same words my wife used on the phone that night when I was in an Ottawa hotel room 2000 miles away. The same words He speaks to all of us who will listen: "My presence will go with you, and I will give you rest."

6

First Light

The man who reads nothing at all
is better educated than the man who reads
nothing but newspapers.
—THOMAS JEFFERSON

For many years it was my habit to start the day with the newspaper. I savored my customary peanut butter and honey sandwich (lightly buttered) and washed it down with milk while digesting the *Calgary Herald*, a longtime friend who greeted me seven days a week at our front door. As a writer and editor, I need to be aware of current trends and events, I kept reminding myself. And so I spent 10 or 15 minutes each morning dutifully scanning the bulky pages for perceptive quotes, quips, and facts. My wife munched cold cereal nearby, gazing out our dining room window, talking to the kids, or asking me questions I sometimes answered.

One day a certain truth began to dawn on me. "Honey," I said, "Listen to this." Ramona listened as I read the following headlines which were *all* on page three:

- Car bomb kills 21 in Russia
- Man dies in fire
- Smuggling ring's suspected boss nabbed
- 20 die after plane crashes on island
- Thousands protest nuclear waste move
- Police arrest six in pedophile plot

- Bus plunges into ravine killing 14
- Desire for revenge sparked beating

Folding the newspaper and tucking it into the bottom of the birdcage, it occurred to me that my habit of starting the day this way was contributing to my rising stress level. And hindering my search for peace. Yes, the world is a tragic place where bad things happen. We dare not hide from the fact. But several questions came to mind:

- Does the news spark compassion, prayer, and generosity, or an icy numbness within me?
- What did past cultures miss by not knowing what occurred a world away?
- What benefit can we possibly receive from a daily diet of bad news?
- Is this really news or merely a compilation of what editors who need to sell newspapers think people will read?

I made a decision that day to save the newspaper for later. I still read it, but I don't start the day with it, nor do I let the sun go down with the news. If I skip a few weeks, chances are I didn't miss a thing. In fact, sometimes the best news is no news at all.

When I was a boy my mother told me numerous times, "Son, you are what you read. So don't read more than one Archie comic book at a time."

I don't get legalistic about this, but I'm learning to start the morning differently. I start with thanksgiving—for a new day, for the strength to open my eyelids, for a dog that has probably pounced on me by now, licking my face and sneezing in my beard. I'm learning that my circle of concern may be as large as the world, but my circle of influence is limited to only a few people. I'm learning to spend my time with the few, modeling compassion and integrity.

I'm learning that time spent reading the Bible is time I'll never regret. And so I make those the first pages I open each day. On one of those mornings, I noticed these words a busy king by the name of David wrote a few thousand years ago:

> Let the morning bring me word of your unfailing love, for I have put my trust in you. Show me the way I should go, for to you I lift up my soul (Psalm 143:8).

I'm beginning to understand that the early hours are of particular importance in shaping our day. Morning is a holy time. A chance to start again. A time to expect the best from God. An opportunity to search for and focus on the good news.

Jesus understood this well. Mark 1:35 tells us that "Very early in the morning, while it was still dark, Jesus got up, left the house and went off to a solitary place, where he prayed." The disciples were surprised that He was gone. They went looking for Him. When they finally found Him, they exclaimed, "Everyone is asking for you." Though I'm no Greek scholar, I imagine Peter scolded Jesus for turning off His cell phone. "Everyone's trying to get a hold of you," he said, wagging his finger. "People back in Nazareth want you to speak at a fundraiser. There are things to do, crowds to impact, people to heal. Didn't you get the message I left on your answering machine? And what about my e-mail?"

Jesus merely smiled at the disciples. He knew that they would one day understand the stress of public life, and He hoped they would learn to start the day in the very best place—on their knees.

Another habit fell soon after this one.

In those days my first act upon arriving at my office was to turn on the computer and check my e-mail, then start straight into my list of phone calls to return, projects to finish, letters to write, reports to compile. Americans download 11 billion e-mails a day, I'm told, and sometimes I felt like half of them came through my modem. And so I slowly learned to leave the computer off for an extra five minutes or so. The transformation in my day has been noticeable. I usually spend time reading a short meditation from Oswald Chambers' *My Utmost for His Highest,* an old book that sat unopened for too long. Or I read a chapter from the Bible. Then I pray for the people closest to me; their names are written reminders on a small sheet that is now a bookmark. If I skip a few days I don't sweat it. But I miss it. And when I remember to practice this small discipline, my day is brighter, my mind sharper, and my spirit right.

Pause

Actual newspaper headlines:

> Dentist receives plaque
> Girl becomes Methodist after delicate operation
> Cemetery allows people to be buried by their pets
> Local high school dropouts cut in half
> Father of nine fined $100 for failing to stop
> Kids make nutritious snacks
> Hospital sued by seven foot doctors
> Obesity study looks for larger test group

> My pace of life has decreased over the past five years, partly because we hardly watch television. We go to bed early and wake up early. We read to each other before sleeping. We laugh more. We hang out around the house when we can. We spend time making meals together more than going to restaurants. We slice tomatoes, grind spices, and separate the beans by hand. We look each other in the eyes while speaking much more than we used to when on the run. And we find that a sparkle has returned to them.
>
> —PAUL STEINHAUER

Being able to read more has slowed me down. I have always been a bookworm. When my youngest hit junior high, I slowly went into the work force. Even though I worked in a library cataloguing books, I had less time to read. During the last year or two, I have taken time to sit and read again. It is most satisfying to be able to read for an hour or two again.

—CAROLYN GRAHAM

After years of being a homemaker, I had to return to the workplace. Suddenly life became very hectic for me, often leaving me feeling frantic and frenzied. I desperately needed a place to unwind. A place I could call my "alone spot." Finding a corner in our home that has deep windowsills and windows on three sides, I made room for my peaceful stuff: a rag doll, dried flowers, candles, pictures, and magazines in a pretty basket. Now, when I am rushing, inside and out, I retreat to this room, light a candle, sit down, take a deep breath, and talk to God. It is here I find tranquillity. It only takes a few minutes, but it helps me face the rest of the day in an unruffled manner.

—ROSALIE GARWOOD

In the morning, O Lord, you hear my voice; in the morning I lay my requests before you and wait in expectation.
—PSALM 5:3

**Great is his faithfulness;
his mercies begin afresh each day.**
—LAMENTATIONS 3:23 NLT

7

The Kingdom of Noise

Noise proves nothing. Often a hen who has merely laid an egg cackles as if she had laid an asteroid.
—MARK TWAIN (1835–1910)

I came home from work one day to discover that my house was moving. My sons had commandeered my stereo and had broken the sound barrier with music that sounded like a horde of angry cats chasing a bagpiper. I smiled as I approached the house, knowing that what goes around comes around. You see, throughout my teenage years I gladly drove inexpensive cars if they had expensive stereo systems. Noise was a big part of my life back then. I put on the headphones at night and fell asleep somewhere between Chicago and the Eagles. Sometimes I miss the good old days. But more than anything, I miss my hearing.

The League for the Hard of Hearing reports that I am not alone. Noise is the leading cause of hearing loss in the 28 million people with impaired hearing in the United States, and the patients are younger than ever. Pete Townsend of the rock group The Who has tinnitus from performing before huge crowds and large speaker towers for the past three decades. "I can't even hear what my children are saying," he said recently.

We not only live in a fast-forward world, we live in an excessively noisy one. One day I stood in a cafeteria line

46

beside a teenager who had surgically implanted headphones just above his earrings. I smiled at him and then mouthed a question. Kindly removing the headphones, he cocked his head.

"Are you okay?" I asked. "It sounds like someone's killing chickens in there." I was thankful he smiled too. "I'm listening to Blink 182," he said proudly. Then he laughed and shook his head. "Killing chickens," he said, sliding the headphones back into place and turning up the chickens.

Noise-induced hearing loss, as the experts call it, is by no means a new problem. Ancient papyrus from Egypt shows that men working near Nile waterfalls developed it. So did those working in print shops, shipyards, and church nurseries. But in the last 20 years the culture of noise has descended on North America with a vengeance. Movie theaters have pumped up the volume. Bands at wedding receptions are tired of being background music. Boom boxes on city streets and earsplitting rock-and-roll performances are the norm. "Every part of our environment has increased its noise," states Dr. Marin Allen, who studies such things. She cites an increase in urban traffic, heavy equipment, and the use of power tools. "Everything we do seems to be louder," she says. "If you use a hair dryer next to your ears for a period of years—you know that's something that our grandmothers didn't have. That's part of life now."

All of us seem to be affected by an addiction to noise. But perhaps we are losing something even more valuable than our hearing. It is our ability to listen. To quietly contemplate. To be still and think deeply.

In C.S. Lewis' *The Screwtape Letters,* wicked Uncle Screwtape boasts, "We will make the whole universe a noise. The melodies and silences of Heaven will be shouted down in the end." Richard Foster, the author of *Freedom of Simplicity,* agrees: "Our Adversary majors in three things," he writes, "noise, hurry and crowds. If he can keep us engaged in 'muchness' and 'manyness,' he will rest satisfied."

Some of us are fearful of silence. If we stop and listen, we may not like what we hear. We find solitude synonymous with loneliness. And so we miss the quiet whisperings of God. Though He can be heard anywhere, He speaks most often in the silence, rarely through our headphones and seldom during traffic jams. As surely as light makes no noise as it travels, God is best heard where noise does not distract and disturb and interrupt. "Where the river is deepest," says an old Italian proverb, "it makes the least noise." We are deepened in the quiet places.

The Bible has much to say about the merits of quietness: "Be still, and know that I am God" (Psalm 46:10), "In quietness and confidence is your strength" (Isaiah 30:15 NLT), "My sheep recognize my voice," said Jesus in John 10:27, "I know them, and they follow me" (NLT).

Such following cannot take place without listening for directions.

I once asked a teenager who was voted most popular girl in her entire high school what her secret was. She said simply, "I listen."

No one loves a good movie or a loud celebration more than I, but there are times when we must be still and listen. When we would do well to drive with the radio off. Or watch a birdfeeder rather than a television.

Now I'd better go and try to convince my sons to pull the plug on the kingdom of noise.

8

Insomniacs Anonymous

A field that has rested gives a bountiful crop.
—OVID (43 B.C.–A.D. 17)

I don't know about you, but I am sick and tired of insomnia. I am tired of feeling as if I've been studying for a math exam when I wake up in the morning. The people who study such things tell us that 48 percent of North Americans suffer from some type of sleeping disorder. If that's true, we need to stay awake until we think of a cure. And that's precisely what I've done. Here are ten quick tips that I've been compiling between midnight and two o'clock in the morning. Ten tips that will help you sleep like a rock—not wake up feeling as if you've been under one.

1. Learn your speed limit. True, Leonardo da Vinci, Winston Churchill, and Florence Nightingale each slept only four hours a night, but mere mortals such as you and I need more. According to the experts, the average North American gets about 8.1 hours of sleep a night. (The average father gets 7.7 and the average mother 7.9—I thought that would interest you.) Find out what your body requires and do your best to get it.

2. Get more exercise. A recent Stanford University Medical School study shows that older and middle-aged people sleep substantially better when they add regular exercise to their routine. You sweat less at night if you do so during the day. One caution: Before you go to bed, wait at least three hours after exercising so your body has time to unwind. Unless you are in your teens. If you are, you are in your prime sleeping years. Don't forget to set your alarm clock for three o'clock tomorrow afternoon.

3. Don't go to bed hungry. Ever wonder why you can't get off the carpet after Christmas dinner? Chemicals in turkey, milk, tuna, cottage cheese, soy nuts, chicken, pumpkinseeds, and cheese can cause drowsiness. Do not eat these before church and rarely eat them all at once. Avoid large helpings of chocolate cake or drinks that may have caffeine. Refrain from chewing coffee beans.

4. Make your sleeping area comfortable. Decrease the noise and light in the bedroom as much as possible. Remove the telephone or turn it off. Place your cell phone in the sink. White noise can be created with a small fan or a soft tape or CD. If snoring is a problem, buy earplugs. Wear a sleep mask if necessary. Take it off before you go to work the next day.

5. Move your clock. If one is staring at you in the middle of the night, it will only remind you that you aren't sleeping. Worrying about sleep is enough to keep anyone awake.

6. Control the thermostat. Your room should be a comfortable temperature. Sixty-eight degrees is ideal for most people because body temperature drops during sleep. If you can blow smoke rings with your breath, turn up the heat.

7. Be consistent. As much as possible, stick to the same general bedtime and waking time every day—even on weekends. If you can, bring your pillow on trips. Leave your bed at home.

8. Take time to wind down. Remember you can't land a Boeing 747 on a 60-foot runway. Your body, too, needs time and space between a hectic day and bed. So consider a warm bath, a hot shower, prayer, conversation, or a good book before bedtime.

9. Sleep like a baby; don't act like one. If you get angry about not sleeping, you will not sleep. So don't go to bed to do your taxes, figure out your business strategy, or rescue endangered species. Associate bed with sleeping.

10. Learn to trust. Scripture verses in the middle of the night can turn the worst experience into a good one. David, a charter member of Insomniacs Anonymous, wrote, "On my bed I remember [God]" (Psalm 63:6); "I will lie down and sleep in peace, for you alone, O LORD, make me dwell in safety" (Psalm 4:8).

Should these suggestions fail you, remember that even insomnia can be a blessing. Though I have little quiet time in my hectic day, I do have the nights. Insomnia has provided me ample time to meditate, to pray for others, and to consider the quiet voice of God, who whispers, "Go to sleep my child. Your Father is awake."

Now it's time to shut off the computer. And set the alarm clock for tomorrow afternoon.

YOUR MOTHER AND I ARE FEELING RATHER STRESSED OUT
RIGHT NOW – LOOKS LIKE YOU KIDS WILL HAVE TO RAISE YOURSELVES.

9

Stressbusters 101

Stress may be the spice of life or the kiss of death.
—ROBERT ELLIOT, CARDIOLOGIST

We all deal with stress in different ways.

I recently read of a New Zealander who had a small disagreement with a clerk at his bank. They exchanged some heated words, and the New Zealander went home stewing about it. The next day he returned to the bank with a brown paper bag, paid for a safe-deposit box, and locked the bag in the box before leaving with a wide grin. Some people rob banks, this man left something.

The bag contained no money or valuables. Just a fish that was growing riper by the minute.

Things went along just fine at the bank for the next 48 hours. Until the clerks began sniffing the air and customers looked at each other with questioning glances. Finally the bank had to be closed and the safe-deposit boxes dismantled one at a time until they found the culprit.

Here in Canada a stressed-out Oshawa woman was ordered to pay her neighbor $11,000 for subjecting her neighbor to 43 harassing acts over three years, including lobbing dead birds onto her property. "This is an extraordinary tale of neighborly misconduct," Justice John Sheppard said in a judgment. Anne Rudka engaged in an "unbelievable and outrageous" campaign against her neighbor. The incidents included "keying" the neighbor's car, leaving a note laced with expletives, lobbing eggs onto the property, leaving letters commenting on the neighbor's clothing, placing numerous calls and hanging up, nailing a note on the property stating that the neighbor and her husband neglected their dogs, pouring acid on the husband's car, trying to set fire to their fence and spray-painting it gold, spraying their dog with Varsol—a paint thinner—threatening to contact Revenue Canada (Canada's equivalent of the IRS), and using a dog whistle to harass their pets.

Stress, these neighbors would agree, is rarely a funny thing.

I asked some authors, educators, homemakers, and ministers what they do when life seems too jam-packed, when road rage beckons, when they feel like spray-painting something or leaving a bass at the bank.

I think you'll enjoy their answers.

❋

I handle stress very well. Of course, I've been in the bathtub since last Sunday night.
—MARTHA BOLTON

One of the things that has released much pressure from our lives is not watching television. We are bombarded every day by so much misery and sadness that we grow numb. At first it sounds selfish, but it has not made us that way at all. Instead, my prayers are more specific now, and I am not overwhelmed by information that I have little control over and which, in the end, often ends up just making me angry. I am still informed but I am not overwhelmed.
—CAROLYN AARSEN

Sometimes I envy my cat. She has time for the small things. Like stopping to eat the flowers.

—SHERRIE ROBINS

In my particular line of work, life is run by a schedule. So I schedule time away. My wife and I tagged a few days of relaxation onto a trip to Bangkok. We went to the ocean and had time to reflect, shop, and talk.

—ELDON BOLT

After more than a quarter century of teaching every Sunday school class, Awana club, and Bible study in sight, and after baking all the cinnamon rolls and entertaining all the visitors that come through town, I am learning that what people demand of me and what God requires are not always synonymous. I have learned to whittle away at extra commitments, committee meetings, and activities for which I have absolutely no gifts. To say no and not feel guilty afterward. There is little so urgent that it cannot be dealt with a few hours later.

—JEANETTE WINDLE

Sometimes I have to write on the calendar "STAY HOME!" Then, if someone asks if I have plans, I can give an honest answer. My plans are to stay home, rest, spend time in prayer, or whatever else the day requires.

—CINDY BARNETT

While teaching in a Bible college, I used to talk to the students about the "race" of Hebrews 12:1

and say that God needs fewer sprinters and more marathoners. Speed and rapid burnout too often go together. In most cases the Lord is better served by the steady plodders.

—BOB COTTRILL

Being the head of a publishing business is a two-edged sword: it provides the opportunity to set your own hours, either too many or too few. There are times I need to put in long hours because of deadlines; however, I could work 16 hours a day and there would still be more to do. I've tried to put things in balance and perspective. If I want to attend an important chapel at my son's school, I do it. Sometimes it means that I must work on Saturday to make up for it, but at least I didn't miss one of life's important events. During the summer months, I put in a solid morning of work and sneak away to the golf course in the afternoon to smell the roses, or the trees, or the sand bunkers.

—MIKE KOOMAN

I quit looking at life in terms of years and started looking at it in terms of days. Hours. I didn't want to just keep collecting date book after date book—1999, 2000, 2001—and wonder where the time went. So I changed my focus. I still make long-term plans, of course, but I live in the now. I spend more time appreciating today than planning for tomorrow. We can't have yesterday back, and we've no guarantee of tomorrow. Today is all we really have. I'm learning to slow down and enjoy it.

—MARTHA BOLTON

I was forced to begin slowing down a year ago when the episodes of an irregular heartbeat, which I've had since my teenage years, began to occur more frequently. After spending a day in the emergency ward, then another night and a day in the hospital for a heart catheterization, it was determined that there was nothing physically wrong with my heart—that they could find. The doctors asked me about stress. I realized that the most stress I experience each day was trying to get to work on time (I'm not a morning person!). So I asked my boss if I could arrive at work half an hour later. It's amazing how that extra half hour in the morning allows me to slow down. I try to sit for that half hour and spend more time with the Lord, reading the Bible or a devotional book and praying for my workday before it begins.

—ENID SANDFORD

One thing that motivates me to get things under control is my health. I have three chronic life-threatening conditions: cancer (which is in remission), type II diabetes, and hypertension (high blood pressure). If I slow down now I am much more likely to have more years to live and to serve God in a less frantic way. In Numbers 8:25, the Levites were commanded to retire at 50, so I do feel permission to slow down. That's good news for a pastor like me. When I was lying around recovering from cancer surgery and was told that I'd have better odds buying a ticket on the Titanic, I said I would never get stressed again if I did survive. I lied. But now I'm trying to correct the problem.

—RON MCLELLAND

The Stress Diet

Breakfast
    1 orange
    1/2 slice multigrain toast (lightly buttered)
    1 cup bran cereal
    6 oz. skim milk

Midmorning snack
    8 oz. iced tea

Lunch
    6 oz. lean chicken
    Leaf of lettuce
    8 oz. water
    Small cluster of grapes
    Small scoop of ice cream

Midafternoon snack
    Mix handful of peanuts, 1/2 lb. of fudge and a box of
    chocolates into remaining ice cream. Finish carton.

Dinner
    1 large pizza (loaded) with extra cheese
    1 medium pan lasagna
    Gallon of root beer
    2 raspberry cheesecakes (eat with your hands)
    More pizza
    More ice cream

Bedtime snack
    3 packages Rolaids

Lord,

Keep me from overestimating
my own importance in the grand scheme of things.
Remind me that Jesus took time:
To hold small children on His lap.
To sleep in a storm-tossed boat.
To withdraw from the crowds.
And still He changed the world.
Thank You that Your yoke is easy
and Your burden light.
Lead me beside still waters.
Restore my soul.
May I draw my strength from You.
And spend my life bringing Your peace
to others.

Amen.

PART TWO

Living on Less and Learning to Love It

He who buys what he doesn't need steals from himself.

—Swedish proverb

Give generously, for your gifts will return to you later. Divide your gifts among many, for you do not know what risks might lie ahead.

—Ecclesiastes 11:1-2 NLT

10

Stepping Down the Ladder

There are two ways to get enough:
one is to continue to accumulate more and more.
The other is to desire less.
—G.K. CHESTERTON

Out our dining room window, across a mile of wheat field and two miles of pasture, lies a small cottage wedged within a pine forest where the ground is covered with slick green needles and dotted with animal tracks. A few years ago, Harold and Debbie Leo resided in the cottage with their four sons—energetic coyotes who hunted and hollered and dreamed of mischief.

Late at night when the hollering died down, it was quiet there.

So quiet you could take your coffee to the front porch and listen to conversations a mile away.

But a few years ago, the Leos grew restless. The cottage was a rental, and all their friends were buying houses. Getting ahead. So they found their dream house in town, complete with south windows and a wood-burning fireplace. The mortgage payments seemed reasonable, and Debbie easily got a job. But before long the nightmares began. Increased heating costs, rising taxes, and their children's schooling turned the end of each month into a guessing game, with the score rarely in the Leos' favor. Though they were able to manage, their blood pressures increased with the arrival of each bill. Time together grew scarce.

"A few months ago we sat down in the kitchen," Harold told me, "and we talked about what would happen if we sold our house and moved back to the country. At first the idea seemed ludicrous, but the more we talked, the more it made sense."

The dream house with the south windows sold within a month, and though the cottage in the pine forest is occupied by someone else, Harold and Debbie have found a place a little closer to town where the price is right. With a good set of binoculars we can watch them sipping cappuccinos on their front porch. Not that we'd ever do that.

This past Sunday afternoon following a rainstorm, our whole family set off across the wheat field. It seemed like a good idea at the dinner table, but slogging through the mud, I began to reconsider. To our tiny dog, the grass was towering and the length of the walk daunting. Partway there, the kids turned just in time to watch me slide down a sharp incline—on the seat of my pants. It was funnier for them than for me. They laughed until their little bodies hurt. My big one hurt worse. In fact, it took about a mile for me to see the humor in the situation. Some things are only funny later.

When we reached the Leo house, two dogs greeted us, their tails tapping to some unknown rhythm. Four boys weren't far behind.

Sipping juice in a newly decorated living room, we talk about their step down the ladder, and I find myself wondering if I should tell Harold about the mud on the seat of my pants.

"We did the math and the numbers looked good," says Harold, "but we both agreed that the one thing holding us back was pride. What would others think? What would they say? And then we decided: Who cares? How do you put a price tag on peace?"

"We weren't used to the noise," says Debbie. "I guess some people love it, but not us. We're country folk. If people honk at us, we think they want to stop and talk."

"We couldn't believe how much we were complaining," echoes Harold. "We felt strained and hurried and out of breath. Then we realized we do have some control. We made choices to get there, and we could make choices to get out of there. We were not helpless."

The Leos are part of a growing number who are stepping down the ladder, simplifying life one step at a time. Things aren't perfect, they are quick to admit, but much of the stress is gone.

Simplicity of life is not simplicity of mind. As Richard Foster wrote, "Christian simplicity...allows us to see material things for what they are—goods to enhance life, not to oppress life. People once again become more important than possessions. Simplicity enables us to live lives of integrity in the face of the terrible realities of our global village."

"We've been asking ourselves how we should spend the last half of our lives," says Harold. "We could both have jobs for the next 20 years and salt away a lot of money. But what would we really have when we retire? If the last five years are any indication, we might not have each other."

Debbie smiles and gently punches his shoulder. The sparkle has returned to her eyes as surely as the Canadian spring has pushed through the long months of winter. This spring she planted a garden for the first time in years. In a few weeks they will enjoy fresh salad they don't have to shop for, corn and tomatoes they will pick by hand. Already flowers are springing up outside the front door, their eager faces turned toward the south sun.

"The one thing we do have is today," says Harold, "so we'd like to be able to enjoy it."

After spending some time in Africa, Harold realized that the level of unhappiness in affluent North America is at least as great as in poverty-stricken countries.

"We have such freedom in this culture to do what we want," says Harold. "But freedom can be a painful thing. We have the freedom to compile a huge debt and live under the weight of it for years. We couldn't afford to do that. There's nothing left over for spontaneous fun or helping the needs of others. When we weren't using our time to get money, we were using our time to count or spend it. It was too much for us." Then Harold laughs. "Sounds a little corny I know, but we've cut back our level of living and increased our level of loving." And Debbie punches him again.

Ecclesiastes 4:8 describes a man who worked hard yet was disillusioned. "For whom am I toiling?" he finally asks himself, "and why am I depriving myself of enjoyment?"

The Leos asked themselves the same questions and found the answer. Sitting with them that day, I realized that for many a step down the ladder can be a step to freedom—and a step up in every other area of life.

11

Building the Perfect Chicken

*In a consumer society there are inevitably
two kinds of slaves: the prisoners of addiction
and the prisoners of envy.*
—IVAN ILLICH

I must admit that I like stuff. Always have. Winters of my childhood were characterized by dreams of Christmas morning and sitting on the heat vent drooling my way through the toy section in the Sears catalog. In fourth grade my parents bought me the grooviest pair of flared pants I had ever seen. They were purple with wide vertical stripes. The stripes were bright orange. I was the envy of every kid at Prairie Elementary School. Until Stan Kirk showed up with bigger flares and brighter stripes. In ninth grade I traded a summer's earnings for my very first stereo—a small amplifier, two speakers, and a state-of-the-art record player complete with strobe light. By September I had sold it so I could upgrade. In November I did it again. Then I sat listening to the Eagles' reminder that some fine things have been laid on our tables, but we only want the ones that we can't get.

Each of us seems to be born thirsty for the things we do not have. Advertisements catch our eye. New cars turn our head.

Can we ever reverse the trend? Better yet, is it reasonable to assume that we can really find enjoyment in an uncluttered life?

My compact disc player expired a week after the warranty. "Throw it away," a salesman told me. "It's cheaper to buy another than fix the old one." As I placed the new one in the backseat I realized that we do the same thing with friendships in this culture—and with marriages. Once home, I took the old model to the shed. There I placed it with the other rusting relics, stood there smiling at all the stuff I used to covet, and remembered my childhood.

I was raised below what our government deems the "poverty line," and I must admit, I didn't much like it. "Poverty is hereditary," my dad once joked. "I got it from my kids." The truth was, Dad had turned down a lucrative job offer to enter a nonprofit ministry. He had no idea how nonprofit it would be.

When I was just a boy I took to stealing, hoping to enjoy the same candies I saw my friends eating. I primarily stole from my brothers and my mother, who left spare change in handy places. My brothers often promised me a nickel if I got lost, and they never paid up, so I reasoned I had it coming. When Mom found out what I'd done, I had something else coming—believe me—but that's another book altogether. One day during Sunday school, I invited David Porr to my birthday party, with one condition: that he give me his offering money right then and there. I am not proud of this. I'm just wondering what I did with the fifty cents.

Some spend much time longing for those "good old days" when money was scarce and love was plenteous, but I do not. I give thanks for a happy and uncluttered childhood, but I do not travel the world talking about the benefits of poverty or the merits of theft in Sunday school. At the same time, I have discovered that one of the quickest ways to speed up and complicate our world is to crowd it with stuff.

We are doing this at a record rate.

Today there is one automobile for every 1.7 people in the United States. In China there is one for every 600.

North Americans consume twice as many goods and services per person as we did at the end of World War II. We buy twice as many cars, telephones, appliances, and cheeseburgers. Our houses are three times the size they once were, and we work harder than ever to fill them with stuff. Our economy is fueled by greed, and we are standing at the pumps eagerly squeezing the nozzle.

If we love anything more than money these days, it is approval. The only thing worse than the debt on our new car is the fear that no one will notice when we drive up in it. If I could summarize the honest feelings of many who pursue toys, perhaps it would be this way:

> We just bought a new van, and I am so happy to be in it and to drive around and smell the new seats. It is so clean it doesn't need an air freshener, and the engine purrs like the tiniest kitten. The doors and windows shut like ziplock bags, and the windshield is spotless. The stereo is crisp, the brakes don't squeak, and the tires hug the corners like they're saying good night.

> I am so happy; I think I need another one.

> On Saturday a friend bought a van just like mine. He says he paid less than I did, and there's more flexibility in the seating and one more door on the side. Three days ago my daughter spilled milk on the floor of my new van. Milk that was best before Thursday. Someone scratched the side of my van while I was shopping—a tiny scratch, I

know—but if I find the one who did it I will have
some things to say.

Happiness is nice, but right now I'd settle for
revenge.

I spent an hour in a multimillionaire's mansion in California. He had servants by his pool and guards by his gates. For much of the hour he told me how expensive things are and how he really can't afford what he has. I asked him why he has it. He paused for a minute, then said he didn't really know. "I guess I never had anything when I was a kid," he said, furrowing his brow. "I didn't want my children growing up that way." Seems we never weary of wanting what we do not have. We've never owned more stuff, but it is increasingly difficult to meet a wealthy man who says he has enough. "It's stressful wondering which country we should visit next," he told me.

In a Macy's department store window last year was an advertisement for perfume. Savor the words:

> You want it. You want it bad. Sometimes so much
> it hurts. You can taste it. You feel like you would
> do anything to get it. Go further than they'd suspect. Twist your soul and crush what's in your
> way. Then you get it. And something happens.
> You become the object of your desire. And it feels
> incredible.

Does it really?

A thousand times a day images bombard our minds, creating necessities for us, reminding us that we are unhappy, that we do not have enough. "You do not eat steaks like the ones we serve," the images boast. "You do not live in a Victorian mansion or drive a blue Mercedes like this one. You are not happy because you do not lounge around in silk pajamas like the couples in this catalog. You poor thing. You do not have a television as large as this one or coffee beans that are this freshly brewed. You do not eat bronzed chicken in a perfect kitchen with perfect lighting and perfect children who laugh at all your jokes while the black Labrador retriever lies at your feet flealess and grinning."

What the images really sell us is discontent. Companies spend billions selling unhappiness. And we buy it at a handsome price.

Contrast such a message with the life of Jesus: "You know how full of love and kindness our Lord Jesus Christ was," wrote Paul in 2 Corinthians 8:9. "Though he was very rich, yet for your sakes he became poor, so that by his poverty he could make you rich" (NLT).

In Romans 12, Paul paints a beautiful picture of this rich community of people living in simplicity. They are hospitable people, giving freely to meet each other's needs. They celebrate with those who celebrate and grieve when others grieve. They share, they serve, they trust.

My wife and I have taken to going "nonshopping" lately. Real shopping drives me nuts. I pull into the parking lot of just about any mall in America, and I begin to develop a headache that sinks from my sinuses right down into my wallet. By the time we enter a store with a banner reading "SALE: No Payments Until September!" my eyes can hardly focus.

Lately we've tried something different. We've tried leaving our wallets at home and strolling through a mall counting all the things we do not need. We both enjoy this exercise immensely. Such an attitude counters the discontent sold us on a daily basis and provides freedom. I do not need the silk pajamas or the bright blue car. What I need right now is to hold my wife's hand and repeat these words, "No, we do not have the big-screen television and the perfect children, but we have what you can't sell. We have each other and the wisdom to know that real satisfaction will never come from things, but from relationships—with God first; the others follow. We have the God-given ability to handle our finances with responsibility, with restraint, and with respect for the needs of others. We are rich enough to give some money away. Content to set our hearts on things above."

And when we notice that the grass is looking pretty green on the other side of the fence, we remind ourselves that their water bill is higher.

12

The Crack of the Bat

Money will buy a pretty good dog,
but it won't buy the wag of his tail.
—Josh Billings

I love the game of baseball. The roar of the crowd. The crack of the bat. The taste of the hot dogs. Okay, I'm lying about the hot dogs, but I do love baseball. I enjoy watching grown men play their hearts out for sheer love of the game. Or perhaps the $250 million has something to do with it. When I was a boy I didn't know you could get paid to play a sport. I knew you could get paid to get lost, but not for playing a game. My Little League coaches kept reminding me that they didn't get paid, that they were here on their own time, so we should smarten up, pay attention, and keep our eyes on the ball. Still, I loved the game. In fact, I spent most of my waking moments at Prairie Elementary School either trimming the pigtails on the girl in front of me or dreaming of baseball. If only I could make it to the big leagues, I thought. Ah…if only. But it never happened.

Until recently.

Last September I found myself hanging out with members of Major League Baseball's Toronto Blue Jays. Mike Matheny (who now catches for the St. Louis Cardinals) and I were on a television show together, and after a few minutes of conversation, Mike said, "Why don't you come and have a

HAPPY BIRTHDAY, MOM!

chapel with the team?" I gulped a couple of times, then quickly agreed. Walking timidly through the hallowed halls of the Skydome, I kept asking myself, "What am I doing here? I'm the guy whose fastball travels 13 miles an hour."

"We didn't ask you to come and pitch, Phil," David Fisher, the chaplain, reminded me, "just tell stories."

Though small, the room where we met was brightly upholstered for families. Books, videos, and children's toys were stacked neatly, making it a welcome spot for the players' wives and little ones during home games. One by one the players filed in, kindly shook my hand, and introduced themselves. I already knew their names. After David told them who I was, I nervously began. "I wanted to be like you guys—a professional athlete," I confided. "And I probably could have made it except that I lacked...well, the body and the coordination."

They laughed their approval.

Surrounded by millionaires, I spent 15 or 20 minutes telling them stories of my life. Of scoring the overtime goal in our championship hockey game—zipping the puck right into my own net. Of the joys of rearing children and the richness of relationships. Tears rolled down the face of one famous pitcher as I described my wife's battle with seizures and how the valley of shadows had drawn us closer to God. And to each other. I told them of my faith in Jesus, not a stuffy religion, but a vital relationship that impacts everything I do and say. It wasn't very polished, but they voiced their appreciation.

Then came the questions. How do we make our lives rich without spending money? "Give it all to me," I joked.

Afterward, Mike, a fellow believer and now a friend, asked me how many children I have. I should have told him 11, but being a good Christian, I had to tell the truth. He disappeared for a few minutes, then returned carrying three autographed baseball bats—one for each of the kids.

"Whoa," I said, "you won't believe how much they'll love these. My eldest son eats, sleeps, and dreams baseball."

That night the Blue Jays began a losing skid. One that eventually cost them the pennant. I don't think it had anything to do with me.

The next day, after managing to get the bats aboard a commercial airliner (you should try this sometime), I carried them through the front door to squeals of delight. At first I thought the kids were glad to see me. But they were looking at the bats. For them, it was Christmas in September.

That night I fell asleep thinking about those bats. And I must admit I thought a time or two of their value, and it brought a greedy smile to my face.

I told a few friends about the bats the next morning, but upon arriving home from work that afternoon, I discovered the two boys in the backyard with the bats, hitting various hard objects (including each other), and generally smudging the autographs. I was not a happy father. I yelled a little at first, then took to hollering. The boys seemed rather surprised at the level of my concern, but I informed them that the bats were worth a whole lot of money, that I could get on the Internet right now and raffle the bats off to pay for their college tuitions, for Pete's sake, but that I wouldn't, that I would instead make the boys labor in an Alaska coal mine while their friends became doctors and lawyers and leaders of the free world. Okay, I didn't say all of that, but I felt like it. And as I was lying in bed that night thinking about the situation, a thought came out of nowhere and smacked me right between the ears: "Phil, those bats are pieces of wood. They will one day burn. Your kids are worth more than that, aren't they?" Pushing the warm covers away, I tiptoed down to the boys' room and did what I've done numerous times since the birth of our first child: "I'm sorry, guys," I said. "I was wrong."

And I slept a little better without the greedy smile.

"Cast but a glance at riches," said Solomon in Proverbs 23:5, "and they are gone, for they will surely sprout wings and fly off to the sky like an eagle."

Henry David Thoreau elaborated this way: "Money is not required to buy one necessity of the soul."

Bats crack. Cars rust. Paint peels. Appliances quit.

But people live forever.

If ever I need a reminder, I tiptoe downstairs into my son's room, pick up some bats, and try my best to read the autographs.

13

The Big Rocks

*A penny will hide the biggest star in the universe if
you hold it close enough to your eye.*
—SAMUEL GRAFTON

An hour ago, Stephen, my 15-year-old son, glanced over
my shoulder and asked me what I was doing. "I'm writing
about living on less and learning to love it," I said. He
squinted a little, then smirked. "Is that possible?" he asked.

Good question. How would you answer?

These days Stephen has taken a summer job. He's saving
for his very first stereo (and perhaps a car, as I'm a little reluctant to let him practice on ours). Living on less and learning
to love it is not really his guiding theme right now. Earning
more and learning to spend it is a little more appropriate.

Through the years, I've connected best with my children
while telling them stories, so I stop writing and ask Stephen
if he has a minute. He nods and slumps into a nearby chair
to listen.

When I was his age, I got my very first paying job on a
farm collecting rocks. Sounds strange, I know, but that's
what the farmer wanted. On a dusty, wind-whipped Friday,
four friends and I trudged behind an old Massey Ferguson
tractor, scouring a furrowed field for stones. We called it rock
picking. Anything bigger than our fist was to be plucked
from the ground and placed in a trailer hitched to the tractor.

The farmer was wise in staying on the tractor and wiser still in choosing young teenage boys. He knew we would try to outdo each other in the macho department to the point where we would find ourselves picking up objects the size of school buses, objects Superman would pretend not to notice. But we were good souls; we did it not only for the pride, but also for the money. You see, the farmer was paying us a whopping three dollars an hour, a monumental sum that caused the sun to shine when it wasn't and my mind to whirl with endless possibilities.

At seven o'clock that night we lined up, and the farmer paid us in cash. I coolly pocketed $30 in fives and returned home the wealthiest kid alive. Sleep took some time arriving that night. For one thing, I was thinking about the size of the wallet wedged beneath my pillow. And wondering if my older brother saw me smuggle it there.

The next day I carried that wallet with me everywhere, just in case I needed to look in it. During an impromptu backyard football game that afternoon, I placed the wallet in my coat pocket and laid it by a poplar tree. All afternoon I tried to keep an eye on the ball, but my left one was on my wallet. Twenty boys in a backyard makes one careful. Twice I went over to the wallet, just to check if the money was still there and to run my fingers through it. Of all the backyard football games I have ever played, this was perhaps the least enjoyable. I missed tackles, dropped passes, and fumbled in the end zone. I jumped too soon, arrived too late, and tackled people early.

The last play of the game would have been on every sports show in the country if we had a camera. In the huddle, Roger Pike told me to go long. So I took off running. I zigged when my opponent zagged and left him on his belly, chewing grass. Into the neighbor's yard I raced, trying my best to intersect with Roger's pass. The ball was launched in a high and perfect rainbow arch. I had it in my sights. Then for some strange reason, I took a quick glance to see if anyone was near my wallet. As I did, I ran straight into Mr. Zweifel's mahogany picnic table. Or at least that's what they told me when I woke up in my own little bed. My wallet was beside me. But one of those crisp five-dollar bills was missing. I wonder to this day if Roger took it as payment for that dropped pass.

Stephen smiles widely as I tell him this.

"Sure, it's funny for you," I say.

Twenty-five years have passed, but still I find myself running into picnic tables. I know that deep and abiding satisfaction, peace, and joy come from keeping my eyes on the prize, from sitting up and paying attention to life. But sometimes I take quick glances at the sidelines, just in case I'm missing something.

"Money is a powerful magnet," I tell Stephen.

"It's the root of all evil, right?"

"No. But the *love* of it is."

Matthew Henry's words come to mind: "There is a burden of care in riches; fear in keeping them; temptation in using them; guilt in abusing them; sorrow in losing them; and a burden of account at last to be given concerning them."

I tell Stephen these things, but still there are question marks on his face. How do we keep our eyes on the prize with all the distractions? How do we find joy in simplicity?

Perhaps one more rock story will provide the answer.

A few years ago a college chemistry professor stood to his feet on the final day of class. "Ten years from now most of you won't remember a thing I've said this semester," he told his class with startling honesty. "But I don't think you'll ever forget what I'm about to show you." The students sat up and the class clown quit making faces.

Pulling from beneath his podium a wide-mouthed glass jar, the professor set it on a table for all to see. Then he took a few dozen fist-sized rocks and carefully placed them, one at a time, into the jar. The class was intrigued. When the jar was filled to the top, he asked, "Is this full?"

The class clown stood to his feet and pronounced, "Yes, sir, the jar is full."

Smiling, the professor reached beneath the podium and pulled out a bucket of gravel. He dumped the gravel in the jar and shook it, causing pieces of gravel to work themselves down into the spaces between the big rocks. Then he asked once more, "Is it full?"

This time no one said anything. Not even the class clown.

Still grinning, the professor reached under the table and brought out a bucket of sand. As he dumped the sand into the jar, it too worked its way into the spaces left between the rocks and the gravel.

"Is the jar full?"

"Yes," someone said.

The professor grabbed a pitcher of water and began to pour it in until the jar was filled to the brim. Then he put the lid on and looked at the class. "What can we learn from this about life?" he asked.

Once again the class clown stood. "No matter what, you can always cram more stuff into your life," he said. The class laughed. The professor joined them. "You know," he said, "you've said some dumb things this semester, but nothing quite that dumb. Here's what I want you to remember: Put the big rocks in first, and everything else will fall into place."

Stephen is intrigued by the story.

"You're one of those big rocks for me, son," I tell him. "You see, a few years ago when your mother and I were considering moving to California so I could take a job for more money than you can imagine, we were in an earthquake in Seattle. It shook all the rocks and the gravel and the sand in my life and caused me to write out a little mission statement that guides my decisions."

"What is it?" he asks.

"Simply this: 'I will consider myself a success when I'm walking close to Jesus every day. When I'm building a strong marriage, loving my kids, and performing meaningful work. I'll consider myself a success when I'm making others homesick for Jesus.' Those are the big rocks for me."

Fifteen-year-olds are not known for sitting still, but Stephen is still with me.

"There's nothing like a trip to another country to teach you about those rocks," I tell him. "Do you have time for one more story?"

"Sure," he shrugs.

"Okay," I say, "but you'll have to wait until I write the next chapter."

14

Five Days That Changed My World

The door to happiness opens outwards.
—SOREN KIERKEGAARD

The water changes color as you leave Miami and fly southward. Fingers of emerald thrust upward, searching for sand, enticing tourists, and resurrecting ghosts of pirate ships that sailed these seas a hundred years ago. Last night my wife and I tickled, kissed, and prayed with three excited children, leaving them in the care of gracious friends. "I hope they'll still be our friends five days from now," I whisper as Ramona and I munch an airline breakfast.

The stewardess closes the first-class curtain on us peasants in economy, and I pick up *Angela's Ashes*. It's one of a dozen books I've devoured preparing for this trip, a tale of intense poverty in war-torn Ireland. Behind us sit our hosts, friends from the child development agency Compassion. "We want you to catch a vision of another world," they told me some months ago. "It just may change your life...and your writing." The world they've chosen is the Dominican Republic, the eastern two-thirds of the island of Hispaniola. A world you don't prepare for in books.

From the window of a Boeing 777, the Dominican Republic rises lush and green, a visible contrast to neighboring Haiti, where voodoo has stripped the nation of its forests and its people of hope. We touch down in Santo

Domingo amid heat that could poach an egg, and jostle with tourists who spend $55 a night being pampered by servants and eating from buffets the size of a jumbo jet.

They say successful missionaries pack a good sense of humor and no sense of smell. An hour later I understand why. Everything works on our truck except the horn, which is the weapon of choice for driving here. Noise abounds in this city of 2 million. As do potholes and pickup trucks that seat a dozen. Construction knows only two speeds—slow and stop. Guards ride shotgun outside grocery stores, and small children poke coconuts and mangoes toward those who obey stoplights.

North Americans have money. Dominicans have time.

This is a land of contrasts. The rich breathe easy behind walls of concrete, while their neighbors sift through garbage and drink from murky streams. Scrawny dogs prowl the alley behind the Jaguar dealership. Dogs no one stoops to pet. In our hotel lobby, the vice president of the country fields questions from the media. Upstairs, Bugs Bunny speaks Spanish on channel 11. I click the remote control effortlessly, causing my wife's head to spin. Seventy-four channels and nothing on. "What a world," I tell her. "We tune things out so easily." Tomorrow we won't be able to. Tomorrow we will begin visiting Compassion's projects. As a tropical sun sinks from a neon sky, Ramona and I kneel together and pray, "Dear Lord, keep our kids in Your care. Bless their baby-sitters. And help us hear Your voice tomorrow."

※

The tropical heat hits you first thing in the morning, pasting your clothes to your body by noon. It's an hour's drive to Sammy Sosa's old neighborhood, still devastated by Hurricane George. Sammy is hitting home runs in Chicago this week amid trade rumors. In a tiny church, children smile broadly when I mention his name. "Hola," I say, almost exhausting my Spanish vocabulary. "We're from Canada."

Our interpreter's name is Victor Hugo, a towering Dominican graced with a quick smile and an easy laugh. I am thankful he takes over. "It's cold in Canada 11 months of the year," I say. Victor smiles. "Snow. Ice. Hail. Have you heard of hail?" They shake their heads. I show them pictures of my children and tell them that Jesus loves white children too. We dispense suckers and a bag full of hats, 160 of them. The blue ones are gone first. "Sammy Sosa," the kids are saying. Now they want to sing for us. And they do, with rhythm and life: "Jesus *me ama*...the Bible tells me so."

"We'll speak Spanish in heaven," Victor tells me as we leave the church. "You'd better learn it here." I am searching for my favorite hat. The green one with the cross. "One of those kids stole my hat," I tell him. "Hang onto your wallet," says Victor.

In a neglected shack the size of my garden shed, a weary mother holds suckling twins and offers us the only chairs she has. "Six people live here," says Victor.

"Where's the father?" I ask.

"She doesn't know. He left a few months ago."

Ten minutes away in another world the tourists lounge and laugh and sip piña coladas. Outside the shack, we side-step an open sewer. Shoeless children grin and try to figure out the gifts we bring. "Open them...like this," I tell them, peeling an egg. "Chocolate on the outside, and inside... aha...a surprise, *amigos!*" The children squeal with delight, their lips covered with sweets.

A mother hands me the cutest little black baby I've ever seen. His big brown eyes poke holes in my emotions. I hold him, noticing his makeshift diaper and breathing through my mouth. The mother stands shyly to one side as my friends take pictures. "He's the youngest of eight," says Victor. As I hand him back, his mother takes me by surprise. "You take heem, *señor*. I can't feed him...you take heem." My eyes mist over and I cannot speak. She chatters in broken English about giving him a better life. About Canada. I gently hand him to her and walk away. How could she? And then I realize that I can scarcely understand loving a child enough to give him away.

As we climb back into the air-conditioned truck, my mind is awhirl. And my green hat is in my back pocket.

※

An hour away Carlos is worried. Orphaned at five, his face looks older than his seven years. His head is bandaged from a stray rock, his forehead creased. Carlos' neighborhood is infected with typhoid and chicken pox and mumps. Boys sit in the rain, bagging water from a crude hose. Water they will sell at the market, dispensing poison for a peso. A Christian neighbor took Carlos in a few months ago, but the money's running out. He won't be able to attend school anymore, she tells us. Or get a job. Or learn the computer. I'm wondering what my place is in all this. So many needs. So many hurts.

My wife interrupts my thoughts: "You tell him we're going to help," she tells the interpreter. "We're going to sponsor him." Starting tomorrow Compassion will care for his family's medical needs, get them into a church, and train him for a career. It will cost us a cup of coffee a day. Small price to pay for the grin on Carlos' face.

The grin keeps coming as we present him with a leather baseball glove and a ball signed by our children. He tries on the backpack full of gum and toothpaste and stuffed animals. Icing on his cake.

The warm rain falls fast as we attempt to navigate the muddy street. Three inches of red mud on our shoes and we're laughing and slipping and falling. An old man emerges from a bright pink shack. "Come," he motions. We follow. Behind the shack he pours water into a basin and scrubs our shoes and washes our feet. We slip him some pesos. But he shakes his head. From the pink shack Andraé Crouch sings on a tinny radio: "I don't know why Jesus loved me." And I sing along, "I'm so glad He did." The rain on our faces mingles with tears. We came to serve but the tables were turned.

Somehow it seems quieter on the flight home. Five days in another world and things seem different. For one thing, I just told my wife that I'll never complain again. Or say things such as "I'm starving," or "Is there anything to eat around here?" I just vowed to quit clutching my blessings and to spread them around. To dispense hope wherever I can. With my words. With my smile. With my wallet. I'm reminded of A.W. Tozer's words, "You have the right to keep what you have all to yourself—but it will rust and decay, and ultimately ruin you."

In the Minneapolis airport we walk past the Bow Wow Shop, where you can buy T-shirts for your dog and jewelry your cat would be proud to wear. Nearby is a bookstore where people purchase Testamints—candy with a cross, and five-dollar golf balls emblazoned with "I once was lost but now I'm found." This year Christians will spend seven times as much on pet food as they do on missions. We'd rather buy posters about changing the world than change our spending habits.

Five days in another world, and the apostle James' words make more sense: "Pure and lasting religion in the sight of God our Father means that we must care for orphans and widows in their troubles, and refuse to let the world corrupt us" (James 1:27 NLT). Five days in another world have also shown me that I probably won't change the world. But with God's help, I can change it for a child or two.

Somewhere tonight a seven-year-old boy drifts off to sleep, a green hat with a cross on it beside his bed. He may not remember my name, and his head still sports a Band-Aid. But he has a full tummy and maybe even a smile on his face. A smile that comes from knowing that God loves him. And someone out there loves him too. Someone he can't see. Someone he may meet again one day soon.

15

Till Rust Do Us Part

Learn to enjoy things without owning them.
—RICHARD FOSTER

It's a frightening thing to awaken one Sunday and find that toddlers have discovered your car. The red one. The one that never had a scratch. Until now.

"An elderly lady owned her," Honest Ed had informed me on a cloudless day the previous summer, while gently caressing her contoured roof and adjusting his purple suspenders. "She only drove it Sundays, you know. Between the church, her heated garage, and the car wash. Changed the oil after each drive. Triple-undercoated the body. Kept plastic on the seats. Heh, heh, this baby purrs like a Swiss watch. Ticks like a pacemaker. And it's all ready to go. Of course, I'll top up the tank before you take it."

Ed looked as if he'd just stepped off a bad television ad. Nonetheless, I squinted at the paint job and thumbed the corners of my VISA card. I hadn't taken her for a spin yet, but already the wheels were turning.

This was the kind of machine fate has you meet once in a lifetime, and you fall in love immediately, vowing to be true the rest of your days, or until rust separates you. And if for some reason you are an idiot and don't buy it right now, you wake up in the middle of the night, cold and sweating, kicking yourself in the wallet, hoping fate hasn't picked someone else and wondering if you should just hobble on down there right now in your Ford Pinto and sit on the dream until Honest Ed arrives and ties the knot.

"As it is, I'll only be makin' 25 bucks on the deal," said Ed. "It'll go toward crutches for the twins, should they survive the surgery. We've gotta get 'em separated, you know. They're Siamese." A tear wound its way down Ed's pudgy cheek and splashed lightly on his tangerine tie.

There are times when life hands you an easy choice on a silver platter. This was one of those times.

After a short test drive and a long chat with my wife, I bought the car—hook, line, and cruise control. As I eased her out of the lot, Ed gently patted the hood and said goodbye, much like you would if your best friend had just climbed aboard a rowboat and was pointing it toward Italy. "I sure will miss her," I heard him say.

Each Saturday I polished that red Ford.

The chrome rivaled sunshine in those days. We planted tomatoes near it, and they grew fat from the rays. On Saturdays my neighbor Vance would come by to sample the tomatoes and annoy me. "Polishing the tin god, eh?"

I chuckled above my irritation. "Just being a good steward, that's all," I would say. *He's jealous,* I would think. *I don't blame him. How can you blame a guy who's still making payments on a rust-colored '66 Chevy Impala?*

About this time my wife began having children. They came one at a time, unlike Honest Ed's, but as they started to toddle, they would occasionally get together in bunches and hang out near my bright red Ford. This was rarely good news for anyone, least of all the Ford. Sometimes Siamese children aren't the only ones who need separating, you know.

On that fateful Sunday just before the morning worship service, I opened the front door to find Rachael and Jeffrey

IN FIFTEEN COMPLAINTS OR LESS, HOW DID YOUR DAY GO?

standing on the hood, smiling at me. They were two and one, respectively, and both were proud owners of sizable rock collections. Apparently they planned to bring the collections to church, perhaps to put them in the offering, until they were sidetracked by a better idea: *What about we place these atop the shiny red thing and dance on 'em? Maybe we could change it into a two-tone. Maybe we could change Dad into a towering inferno.*

"It's just a *car,*" said my wife as we drove to church, the smell of smoke lingering in the air. The blaze had been extinguished, but a little breeze could stir up the embers. After all, my investment had been devalued, my equity diminished.

"How can you say that? JUST A CAR. It's not *just a car.* It's...it's..."

"Just a car," she interrupted. "Hey, be glad the car didn't decide to trample on the kids."

I wasn't so sure.

Upon reaching the parking lot, I was smiling at other parishioners, but my words were stumbling through clenched teeth. "Look at it this way," I said. "What if the kids scratched your...your...vacuum cleaner or something? Or...damaged one of your plants? Or ripped one of your new dresses?"

"They have, Phil," she said, waving kindly to someone. "By the way, what did you do with the kids?"

※

I don't know if your pastor reads your mail. Mine does. Of course, I don't have tangible proof of this. But even if he doesn't, I highly suspect that our cordless phones are on the same frequency, or that Pastor John spends a significant percentage of his minister's salary on high-tech surveillance equipment that he zooms in on my car, because almost every Sunday he seems to delight in nailing me to the wall.

On the morning in question, his topic was materialism, and before long he was reading from 1 Timothy 6, and I knew I was in trouble.

> But godliness with contentment is great gain. For we brought nothing into the world, and we can take nothing out of it. But if we have food and clothing, we will be content with that. People who want to get rich fall into temptation and a trap and into many foolish and harmful desires that plunge men into ruin and destruction. For the love of money is a root of all kinds of evil....But you, man of God, flee from all this and pursue righteousness, godliness, faith, love, endurance and gentleness (1 Timothy 6:6-11).

Pastor John didn't end there, so I picked up the bulletin and tried to drown out the remaining verses by thinking about auto repair shops and doing mental calculation exercises. The problem was, the verses came through loud and clear.

> Tell those rich in this world's wealth to quit being so full of themselves and so obsessed with money, which is here today and gone tomorrow. Tell them to go after God, who piles on all the riches we could ever manage—to do good, to be rich in helping others, to be extravagantly generous. If they do that, they'll build a treasury that will last, gaining life that is truly life (1 Timothy 6:17-19 THE MESSAGE).

"Martin Luther once said, 'I have held many things in my hands, and I have lost them all; but whatever I have placed in God's hands, that I still possess.' It's funny, isn't it?" asked John. "North Americans possess more things than any other people in the world. We also have more books on how to find happiness."

I was listening now.

"If you hold the things of this world too tightly you will spend your whole life making only a snail's progress toward the Creator," he said. "Things must never fill the place where God was meant to be."

When we reached the car, I wasn't smiling.

"I guess I have some things to learn," I told my wife. "I guess anything we don't give to God has a way of possessing us."

She smiled in agreement. And watched me reach for the car keys.

It was time to let the children out of the trunk.

16

Balancing the Television

*I find television very educational. When it's on I go
into the other room and read a book.*
—Groucho Marx

From time to time I receive flattering letters about my
writing. All of them are from my mother. No, I'm kidding.
But I did have a nice one the other day. It said, "Your book
is just perfect, Phil. It helped us balance our television set."
I was pleased to know that I'd been able to help someone
bring about some balance in their home. Until I read the next
sentence: "Our TV's been a little wobbly since little Billy
chiseled the front leg off. We were looking for something
about a half inch thick. Your book was just perfect."

It's not an easy job, balancing our television sets.

Each year, just after play-off time, my wife and I discuss
the problem that one of us has in this very area. And one of
us agrees to make changes.

I grew up without TV, so perhaps I've spent too much time
making up for it. Growing up without television didn't seem
to affect me in a negative way. Except that I forget some
things. Did I ever tell you that I grew up without television?

My parents didn't allow the thing in our home when I was
a kid. On my eleventh birthday I asked my mother what was
so wrong with television and if she could give me one good

reason why I couldn't have one in my bedroom. She came up with more than one. I believe they were in this order.

1. TV talks too much, but doesn't say enough.

2. TV is violent.

3. TV takes our minds off our minds.

4. You will learn more watching cheese mold than watching television.

"Television is the bland leading the bland," echoed my father from behind the paper. "If the knob marked 'brightness' turned up the intelligence level I'd consider it, sonny. But it's just the opposite. As for me and my family, we will go without."

So we went to our friends' houses and watched their sets.

In ninth grade, on a rainy Sunday evening as darkness began to cast its mantle on our small town, I sat in a friend's living room and watched both hours of *Jaws*, in which a mechanical shark terrorizes a small town. I walked home alone that night, avoiding puddles, vowing that I would not enter a lake or a swimming pool that summer. Nor would I take a bath. And if I had to shower, I would keep at least one eye on the drain at all times.

The experts say that television has no effect on people. I am proof otherwise. I still do not use bubble bath.

People of the Word

According to the *Washington Post*, more than half of all Americans read at least 30 minutes a day ten years ago. Today, only 45 percent do. Even those who read on the Internet are mainly scanning for information without really comprehending what they're reading, says researcher William Albert.

In his book *Amusing Ourselves to Death,* TV critic Neil Postman says that the printed word demands thoughtful analysis, sustained attention, and active imagination. This is not the case with television and video game webzines. They encourage a short attention span, disjointed thinking, and purely emotional responses. If you don't agree, come talk to my children after they've spent an hour with a video game.

As a young man, Postman read the Ten Commandments and was struck by these words: "You shall not make for yourself any graven image." He says he realized that the idea of a universal deity couldn't be expressed in images but only in words. "The God of the Jews was to exist in the Word and through the Word," says Postman, "an unprecedented conception requiring the highest order of abstract thinking."

In a seven-day week, we are given 168 hours. So are presidents, prime ministers, and small children. From a recent survey, here are the top five most popular activities:

Average Guy's Activity Chart

Activity	Time
Sleeping	56 hours
Working	46.5 hours
Watching TV and videos	28 hours
Looking for remote	1 hour
Blaming children for losing remote	5 minutes

The first three on our chart are accurate (we're still researching the others), which should give us cause to stop and listen. The third most popular activity for many today is watching television. And things that enrich our lives, our souls, and our relationships are shuffled to the bottom as a direct result.

A recent study claims that 60 percent of adults believe their lives would be better without television. But how many are actually willing to relegate the TV set to the basement? Very few.

I recently wrote a column called "TV or not TV?" in which I told of our family's agreement to unplug the television for two weeks. The children thought we would die when I suggested it. I *knew* we would. But the results were startling. During those two weeks, I saw changes in my kids. And changes in me. Sure I missed the sports, but for the most part, not watching television freed up time for better things. Things like wrestling with the kids. Reading good books together. Loving my wife. And listening to music. I even hauled out my old turntable and began pulling out old record albums— older readers may remember what these are.

I have spent much of my life a recovering sportaholic. If it bounced, rolled, slid, or flew, I chased it. Or watched it. But during those two weeks even that gum began to lose its flavor. The more I thought about it, the more I realized that my favorite sports team did not mourn when I had a bad day. The more I did other things, the less I missed the commentators on the 24-hour golf channel, whispering, "I think he's taken out a putter, Bob, or perhaps, no…let's see, I think that may be Gatorade."

The sum total of my sports intake has significantly decreased, and I have opted for doing instead of watching. Life is not a spectator sport. Except when it comes to my children's soccer games.

When asked what Christians should do to get out of their superficial rut, radio talk show host Dennis Prager, a non-Christian, responded:

> Stop watching television. Not watching television liberates so much time that I would say it is virtually impossible not to spend the time becoming deeper. Even if you play cards with friends during the time you would ordinarily watch TV, you will be deeper because you are relating to human

> beings. I mean, watching a lima bean grow is a
> deeper activity than watching television.

In the column I encouraged people to paste Psalm 101:2-3 above their televisions: "I will walk in my house with a blameless heart. I will set before my eyes no vile thing." I was unprepared for the reader response.

One man wrote, "I sat down and wrote you an angry letter the night my wife showed me your article. But two weeks later I'm glad I didn't send it. I'm reading again, I'm enjoying my children, and spending time with God."

A lady from Ohio unplugged as well and wrote to thank me. While doing dishes with her son (time normally spent before the TV), he began asking her questions about heaven and hell and Jesus. They knelt together with dishtowels in their hands as he asked Jesus Christ to forgive him of his sins and change him. When he finished the dishes, he went off to tell his sister. And his neighborhood friends.

Several letters seemed to indicate an interesting phenomenon: Unplug the television for two weeks and you may not plug it in again.

Add Six Years to Your Life

None of us is getting younger, and children love to remind us of the fact. Last Christmas I was pulling on a gift—a smaller than usual sweater—when my son Jeffrey said, "It doesn't fit, Dad. But you'll shrink into it. That's what old people do, you know...shrink." It was a not-too-subtle reminder that life moves quickly, that our moments should count.

The average American will spend between 12 and 13 years of his or her life in front of the television. Amazing. Have you ever met someone who said with any degree of honesty, "I wish I would have spent more time with my TV set, or my computer, or my desk"? Likely not. But I've met so many who are spending the last years of their lives regretting the previous ones.

Consider this: If we were to cut our television viewing in half, we would add six extra years to our lives. That's six years of play. Of work. Of noticing a sunset, of walking with a spouse. Of cherishing people and loving God.

Now, I think I'll go plant a lima bean.

17

A Matter of Life and Debt

We will loan you enough money to get you completely out of debt.
—Sign in a loan office

Life, liberty, and the pursuit of just about anything you please. Volvo—a car that cannot only help save your life, but help save your soul.
—Volvo ad campaign

Some time ago, my wife and I sat down at the dining room table to figure out how we were doing financially and whether we could wait until the end of the month to push the panic button. Our net was looking pretty gross, so we decided to list our personal assets. There are two kinds of assets, I'm told. "Liquid" assets are measured by how much you have invested in milk, orange juice, and root beer. "Solid" assets are the ones that will outlive the expiration date on your milk carton. Here was our list of "solid" assets:

- a Shih Tzu/Maltese dog that we paid $300 for (or approximately $100 per brain cell)

- $231.43 in our daily interest savings account (interest 1.4%)

- $220 worth of key chains we have never used

- approximately $13 worth of pop cans

- roughly $700 of spare change beneath our sofa cushions

- $250 in pens in a drawer beside the stove (four of them work)

- $31.50 in postage stamps that we can't use because the Postal Commission raises the rates every other Wednesday

- $176.34 in checking

I may be exaggerating slightly, but it can be startling to sit down and actually list the things the bank doesn't own. If you are about to back your bank-financed car out of your bank-owned garage to drive with credit card gas to open a charge account so you can fill your mortgaged home with new furniture because of a sign that promises "No payments until February," put the keys in your pocket for a minute and read the following. These simple steps have helped my wife and me get out of debt and cut back on the amount we spend on Extra Strength Tylenol.

1. If thy credit cards outspend thee, cut them off. The credit card was first invented by Jacob back in Genesis 25 when he allowed his brother, Esau, to order a meal using MasterCard. Esau, who was deadly with a bow and arrow, but not very good with a calculator, traded in all his rights as the firstborn son on some bread and lentil stew. It was an impulse purchase he and his descendants would regret for years.

Of course, it is possible to use the plastic in your wallet correctly. Here's how: Never buy with credit what you wouldn't buy with cash. If you haven't budgeted for it, don't buy it. The Consumer Federation of America tells us that 70 percent of credit card holders carry $6000 to $7000 in unpaid balances. The interest rates are often more than 20 percent. Furthermore, the average credit card company in the U.S. allows us to borrow 250 percent more than we can afford to pay! So pay your credit card off each month. If you can't, then gather some friends together and have a Plastic Party. See how long a strip you can cut your cards into. Then dip them in candle wax and see how long they'll burn. The loser makes the others lentil stew. How about this for a party theme: "You *can* leave home without it."

2. Earn more than you spend. When our children were old enough to appreciate what money could do, we showed them how to put their small allowance in envelopes labeled, "for God," "for the future," and "for me." If there was more month than money, they learned a valuable lesson. Adults too need to learn the fine art of spending less than they earn.

3. Buy a lottery ticket every 250,000 years. Our government, in its infinite wisdom, has allowed a special tax for people who did not do well in fifth-grade mathematics. It is called the lottery. People who study such things tell us that if you purchase one lottery ticket a week, you have a good chance of winning the jackpot once every 250,000 years. If you still do not understand the mathematics of the previous sentence, please call my fifth-grade teacher, Miss Ida Weismuller. Everything was clearer after she dealt with me. Proverbs 28:20 says, "The person who wants to get rich quick will only get into trouble" (NLT).

4. Choose contentment over consumption. It's amazing what you can spend your money on these days, isn't it? Need a Christmas wreath for the front grill of your car? One that blinks? No problem. How about a gas-powered blender for the backyard? For $365 (including carrying case) one can be yours. Sterling silver thermometer cuff links so you can check the temperature of your wrists? They're available for $98. As I write this, a 1996 Tiger Woods rookie card, which the seller insists is "The Single Greatest Treasure in Existence," could be mine for a cool $600,000. If you have a spare $75 million sitting around you may want to impress your acquaintances with a submarine. Yes, the U.S. government has made them available on the Internet at www.ussubs.com. If that's a little extravagant, why don't you settle for a radar device to divert heat-seeking missiles from attacking your Learjet (I have this happen all the time). It can be yours for a few million.

Obviously, these are extreme examples. But are the things we covet any less silly? The television convinces us that a newer car, a faster microwave, or a smaller cell phone will be just the ticket. Martha Stewart shyly admits to owning 16 televisions. Jerry Seinfeld tries to build garages big enough for his 60 cars. Florida attorney Stacey Giulianti boasts: "I've got a 61-inch TV, which, diagonally, is one inch bigger than my own mother. I've got an 11-speaker surround-sound system. I've got oversized plush couches and a monster-size kitchen with a huge bread maker and a commercial-size mixer. And I've got a large master bedroom with a walk-in closet that is the size of my bedroom in my old house." But the 32-year-old isn't finished. He also has a soaker tub, 12-foot cathedral ceilings, and an enormous Infiniti four-by-four truck that has never been off the highway. "Life is messy," says Stacey, "and it's nice when you're done with your day to be able to come home and soak in the big tub, grill in your big backyard, and watch your 61-inch TV. It allows you to escape the daily stress. You work hard, you want to enjoy your comforts."

Does the accumulation of stuff really help us "escape the daily stress"? In my own experience, I don't tend to own my possessions, they possess me. They cry out to be fixed, to be used, to be replaced. Possessions can consume one of the most valuable assets we have—our time. The fewer things we possess, the more time we will have. Time to invest in people.

5. Remember that your bank does not need your charity. Our bank offers 24-hour banking, which is about how much time it takes me to figure out the bank machine. For each of the last two years our bank has boasted record profits in the billions. I don't know about you, but this is not what I want from my bank. I want my bank to say, "You know, we really didn't make that much this year because we were busy giving you such a great deal." But since banks don't offer that particular service, my wife and I sat down with a calculator and asked ourselves what we could do to give a little less to the bank and a little more to those who need it. This is what we discovered. With interest, our $70,000 mortgage (payable over 30 years) was going to cost us more than $200,000. But if we could find a way to pay an extra $100 a month, we could burn our mortgage and throw glass goblets into our fireplace 15 years earlier. We would also save more than $70,000 in interest. A "payday mortgage" which allows us to make a biweekly or weekly payment will allow us to smash those glasses even sooner. Now all we need is a fireplace.

6. Take the slow boat to the gold rush. During the height of the Internet boom, I wrote out a check (I will not tell you the dollar figures because you will laugh at me) to a company that was listed in the phone book for barely a year. To be honest, my sole reason for investing was the fear of missing out on a huge opportunity some of my friends were getting in on. Greed and envy are among the most common reasons for investing. Our reasons must change. When I invest, I am learning to ask myself, "What will I do if the money is multiplied? What will I do if it is lost?" Investing for future needs—including paying off a house, becoming debt-free, educating our children, and helping others with spontaneous giving—is smart. Investing out of greed or envy is not. If you don't believe this, I have some Internet company shares I'd love to sell you.

7. Plan for the best, but prepare for the worst. When we were first married, my wife informed me one night that her greatest fear was losing me. I was flattered. I said, "Well, I am a pretty handsome guy, that's for sure. Thank you. Thank you very much." Then she reminded me of the reason for her fear. When Ramona was eight years old, a terrible flood devastated the surrounding countryside, claiming the life of her father, who drowned trying to save one of his children. He left behind seven kids and a faithful wife who did everything she could to provide for them. But as Ramona watched her mother work at various businesses (including a peach cannery that paid her five dollars an hour), she found herself fearing that she would be called upon to do the same. One of the first investments we made when our first child was born was a reasonable life insurance policy, ensuring that Ramona would not need to work as her mother had, should something happen to her wonderful—and might I add, handsome—husband.

8. Remember, "new" does not always mean "improved." Though sometimes you buy someone else's problem when buying a used car (dealers call them "preowned" now), more often you save a boatload of cash. In fact, during the average span of your working career, you can easily save more than $150,000 by buying three-year-old vehicles as opposed to brand new ones. The projected life expectancy of the average three-year-old (car, not child) is ten years and 110,000 miles. Many of these vehicles are well-maintained, and motorists who usually go the new car route are now giving serious thought to buying "previously enjoyed" vehicles. New vehicles lose an average of 20 percent of their value the instant you put on the blinker to pull out of the dealership. Some people love the peace of mind of a new car, but I can tell you there is even greater peace in knowing that not a person in the country is going to steal your 1976 Dodge Dart.

9. Put not your trust in retirement accounts. A financial consultant recently met with me to laugh at my financial situation. Actually, he was there to tell me what I would need to put away to live at a comfortable level once retirement came along. The sum was staggering. I am thankful we have already taken certain steps to save for the future, but it is important to remember that there are no guaranteed investments on this earth. Proverbs encourages saving for the future, but we also must remember Jesus' story of the rich fool who ran out of time to spend the money he had stockpiled. God gave the Israelites manna, but instructed them not to hoard it but to eat it, perhaps because of their need to trust in Him daily. Too often such investments can be a safety net in case God doesn't come through, supplying all our needs like He promised to. Jesus challenged us to "store up for yourselves treasures in heaven, where moth and rust do not destroy, and where thieves do not break in and steal" (Matthew 6:20). In 1 Peter 1:3-4, the apostle Peter talked about the only guaranteed and lasting investment: "In his great mercy he has given us new birth into a living hope through the resurrection of Jesus Christ from the dead, and into an inheritance that can never perish, spoil or fade—kept in heaven for you."

Everything we have is God's. Our possessions are a trust from Him. What we clutch tightly, we lose. What we place in His hands, we will possess. Forever.

18

Tales of Simplicity

You must leave your possessions behind when God summons.

—Yiddish proverb

A doctor friend of mine has moved from an eight-bedroom house to a more modest one. His car is ten years old and his hobby is keeping it running. Able to give more than ever to the needy, he recently told me, "I don't gauge riches by the abundance of my possessions anymore, but by the fewness of my wants." Here is how a few other friends and acquaintances have enriched their lives in simple ways:

> When we were newlyweds, our evenings seemed to revolve around doing dishes together. When we got a dishwasher, our evenings began to revolve around the television. We recently decided to give the dishwasher a break three times a week and do dishes together the old-fashioned way, with lots of elbow grease and some old-fashioned towel snapping. I had no idea how much I missed these conversations.
>
> —Deanna Eckart

My motto for this year was to simplify life. Fortunately, I have 218 more days to accomplish it.

—BOB SCHUEMANN

My husband and I go golfing and we leave the scorecard in the clubhouse. I enjoy this time in the great outdoors, and I don't think of anything but the next shot.

—JUDY BLACK

I have been trying to figure out the things that I know I'll regret not doing and make sure I do them. This really helps when I'm trying to decide between two good things. Usually, there's one that I know I'm going to regret someday if I don't do it. Once-in-a-lifetime things usually take the highest priority. Live your life so you have few regrets. I've found that the things that are the most work and drain the most time and energy from my life are those things I didn't really want to do in the first place. Things that I really want to do and really should do don't usually leave me feeling frustrated, even if they're a lot of work.

—MARTHA BOLTON

Chocolate has helped my stress level. Everything looks better after dessert! Not only should we be fed up, we should be prayed up as well. One of my pastors used to suggest that we pray six months in advance of our lives. Pray that we will be walking in grace and forgiveness and learning more what it is to follow Christ. Pray that we will be doing unto others as we would have them do unto us. Life isn't easier or less busy now, but it is covered with grace.

—KIM MOORE

I used to work three jobs to keep up with my lifestyle. Now I have one job, less money, and more time for relationships. I'm not as driven to work to get more money or things. My focus is more on life and living it to its fullest. Now I have more time to be busy!

—JAQUELYN TAYLOR

Living in a small town allows for a slower pace of life. When I go to the big cities, I become panic driven, road rage rules, and the Bart Simpson in me comes out.

—PAUL PERSCHON

My husband and I are in our mid-40s—the sandwich years—with children who are growing up but still need us and with aging parents. My mother started down the Alzheimer's road three years ago. My husband's dad just passed away from a brain tumor, and his mom is schizophrenic and in a group home. Stress is a part of life, but hanging on to the simple pleasures and joys along the way helps shorten the road.

—CAROLYN GRAHAM

Though my life as president of a large publishing house is busy, I find that the very thing I don't have time for is that which relieves the greatest stress. I love to run early in the morning with a group of guys. The fellowship is super and the exercise fantastic. We all run at various speeds and for different reasons, but we all have better health, thinner bodies, and less stress. Physical exercise relaxes me and makes me happier, healthier, and kinder towards others.

—Bob Hawkins Jr.

My husband, Merlin, and I have joined a Monday night Mixed Curling League. This is so slow it's like watching paint dry. We throw our rocks down the ice and then walk back and forth for the next two hours hoping for a chance to hear the skip yell "Sweep!" so we can actually get our blood circulating. Merlin also plays a couple of hockey games each week to prove he is not too old. Although he says it is fast, I have noticed it is a way for him to "slow down."

—Linda McNaughton

When I was newly divorced and had five children at home, living only one day at a time and no more was the only way I survived. God did not give me strength for tomorrow, just today. I wasn't able to do all I wanted for my children, but they look back and know they were loved.

—Doreen Spear

For me, self-employment has provided some additional flexibility to do more of what I want. I'm more in control (or at least I feel so), I realize far greater fruit from my efforts, and I deal with a fraction of the headaches I did before.

—Larry MacClanahan

For the past eight years we haven't had a television in the house. As a result, we are not bombarded with people telling us about all the things we deserve: the goods that always have an emptiness behind the fancy packaging. I remind myself daily of a simple equation: The less I need, the less I need to work. If I don't need the $35,000 vehicle, I don't need to work so hard that year (or the next four years) to get it. I sometimes go for walks along a lovely reservoir in the city, past lovely and massive homes that are well-furnished and empty because both people are away making money so that they can have this lovely home. But when will they have time to enjoy the very things they're working for? We have a lovely home, and I want to be able to sit in it, and be hospitable, and enjoy this good gift God has given us.

—CAROLYN AARSEN

**A man's life does not consist
in the abundance of his possessions.**
—JESUS (LUKE 12:15)

PART THREE

Winning the Race Without Being a Rat

God put me on earth to accomplish a certain number of things. Right now I'm so far behind that I will never die.

—CALVIN AND HOBBES

Fatigue makes cowards of us all.

—VINCE LOMBARDI

Success can go to my head, and will unless I remember that it is God who accomplishes the work, and that he will be able to make out with other means whenever he cuts me down to size.

—CHARLES HADDON SPURGEON

19

Cast Away

*Try not to become a person of success
but rather a person of value.*
—ALBERT EINSTEIN

Here's a question for you. Be honest with your answer. Have you, at least once in the past week, said to someone, "I'm tired"? Perhaps you've said it more than once. Perhaps it's all you've said. Some people don't believe we should ever admit to fatigue, that psychologically the admission will hasten our undoing. But let's face it, we live in Tylenol Times. This is the Aspirin Age. "I'm so tired," someone told me recently, "that if my life was measured in dog years, I'd be dead."

When my son was in first grade I was overwhelmed with a feeling of great importance when it came to my job. Just about every evening I brought home a briefcase bursting with assignments, deadlines, and assorted charts. Believe me, there was nothing brief about this case. One night, as the sun set unnoticed behind our evergreen trees, my six-year-old son sat at the dining room table playing with a fork and watching me work.

Finally he stuck the fork between the table leaves and said, "Dad, what are you working on?"

I told him.

He said, "Oh."

Then he squinted at the fork and said, "Why are you working on it?"

I explained carefully that I had so much to do that I couldn't finish it all during the day.

He squinted even harder at that one, then asked at last, "So why don't they put you in a slower group?"

It would be nice, wouldn't it? This slower group. As it is, the group we're in is anything but slow. According to the U.S. Bureau of Census, there is now a fifty-first state—the state of Concern. One hundred eighty million people claim to live there. We've accessed everything but the pause button. I love cordless phones, but sometimes I think I'd settle for a phoneless cord!

Others insist that we've arrived. Look at us. Technology, industry, commerce—all bursting at the seams. We now have a "Smart Mirror" that scrolls news headlines while we shave or dry our hair. A microwave that connects to the Internet to scan food labels and cook your dinner to perfection. Alarm clocks that regulate temperatures on electronic blankets and activate coffeemakers. A "Smart Sprinkler" equipped to download weather reports and adjust accordingly.

We never cease to amaze ourselves, do we? But have we arrived? I wonder.

If we've arrived, how come my elevator just stopped at all 16 floors without anyone getting on? How come we can't keep bugs from getting in our peaches? At home the other day I opened a can of tomato soup and the lid fell in. Is this progress? We can build space shuttles but we can't get the little red string on the Band-Aid to work right.

In all seriousness, we can get from Portland to Los Angeles in two hours, but we can't get across the street to greet a new neighbor. Our computers are faster, but we've forgotten how to wait. Our cell phones are omnipresent, our dishwashers more efficient, our jets faster. We have bigger houses

HOW CAN I SLEEP WHEN THERE ARE PEOPLE
IN OTHER TIME ZONES MAKING MONEY?

and smaller families. More money and less time. We buy more things and enjoy them less. We've added years to our lives but drained the life from our years. We talk too much, but when do we listen? We have sacrificed better for bigger, peace for noise, e-mail for communication. We have more hype but less hope, more conveniences but less time, more counselors and more problems. We have wider roads and fewer carpools, more information but less knowledge, more choices but less wisdom, taller buildings and shorter fuses. We drink too much, drive too fast, laugh too little, and sleep a whole lot less than we should.

We've doubled our incomes and tripled our divorce rates. We've built beautiful houses and turned them into broken homes. We're stealing time from those who love us and giving it to those who don't. Our schedules are full, but our lives are empty. If this is progress, who needs it?

☀

You can learn much during a four-hour plane ride if you listen. Today I find myself seated next to a friendly middle-aged businessman who is balder than...well...than I. Flipping off his cell phone on cue, he checks and rechecks his watch, then settles back to leaf nervously through the latest issue of *Forbes* magazine. In his right hand is a yellow highlighter pen, and after eagerly using it, he leans my way to show me something. The black letters jump from yellow ink: "Los Angeles drivers burn $800 million a year in gas during traffic jams."

"Incredible," he says with a smile.

"Wow!" I agree.

He continues leafing and highlighting, then points to another statistic. "For the first time in history the 400 richest Americans have a total net worth of $1 trillion, a figure greater than the gross domestic product of China."

"So are we better off?" I ask with a grin.

My question seems to disturb him, resurrecting something deep within. "I don't know," he says slowly.

"I guess I didn't introduce myself," I say, extending a hand. "I'm Livingstone...David Livingstone."

"Oh," he said, "sorry. I'm Robert."

"I was kidding about Livingstone. I'm Phil."

Robert laughs, then wastes little time in telling me his story, a story that will give me plenty to think about for weeks to come.

"Five years ago," he begins, closing the *Forbes* magazine and squeezing it into the pouch in front of him, "I was promoted to the position of vice president of a computer firm. The day I received the news, my wife and I threw a party for several close friends. We had a great time..." Robert is smiling and his voice trails off. Then he looks serious again. "On the way out that night, my best friend from high school shook my hand and said, 'Hey, I'll be seeing you...won't I? You won't get too busy for Saturday mornings, will you?'

"'Of course not,' I told him. 'I'm not about to miss our breakfasts over some job.'"

But the job turned Robert's world inside out. Saturday mornings were spent with his charts and computer. Sunday mornings were a repeat. He never did spend another Saturday morning with his high school buddy. The requirements of the office took priority. One night, six months before our plane ride, Robert came home to an empty house. "I thought I was giving them everything they wanted," he says. "I guess what they wanted most was me."

"Have you seen the movie *Cast Away?*" I ask him.

He hadn't, so I told him about it.

In the film, Tom Hanks plays Chuck Noland, a man who lives his life on permanent fast-forward. As a FedEx executive, Chuck's job is to live life by the clock. To make sure packages arrive on time. To ensure customer satisfaction and accurate advertisements come Super Bowl time. At the start of the film, Noland is seen berating employees in the Moscow field office for missing deadlines. "Let us not commit the sin of turning our back on time!" he hollers. During the Christmas holidays, he is called away from family celebrations to help FedEx solve problems in Malaysia.

Noland's obsessive preoccupation with his watch is his way of avoiding emotional intimacy. His girlfriend does her best to accept a man who is ruled by his beeper. As he dashes to catch his plane, Noland makes an awkward marriage proposal. Without stopping to wait for an answer, he promises, "I'll be right back."

When his cargo plane crashes rather spectacularly in a violent electrical storm, he is, of course, gone a whole lot longer than he expected. With the help of a rubber dinghy, he washes ashore on an uncharted Pacific island. Trapped in a world without clocks, schedules, or a future, Noland's world is paused, caught in a freeze-frame, and almost stopped. As the days stretch into months and the months into years, Noland realizes that he may never be rescued. Desperate for companionship, he begins talking to a volleyball he nicknames Wilson. In the end, only the hope of seeing his girlfriend again gives him the determination he needs to stay alive.

"That's how I feel," says Robert. "Cast away. I guess you don't have to be on some desert island to be cut off from the ones you love."

How true. In a fast-forward world, it's easy to forget the importance of allowing others into our lives and of reaching out to be a part of theirs. It needn't take four years on a desert island to teach us that our lives are more meaningful when we share them with others.

As the plane touches down, I talk with Robert about balancing our work. About the joy it should bring us. I try my best to remember Ecclesiastes 5:19-20: "It is a good thing to receive wealth from God and the good health to enjoy it. To enjoy your work and accept your lot in life—that is indeed a gift from God. People who do this rarely look with sorrow on the past, for God has given them reasons for joy" (NLT).

"If I could just live the last five years over again," says Robert, pulling the *Forbes* magazine from the seat-back pocket and placing it in his briefcase.

"You can't," I say. "But you can change how you live today. I'll pray for you, that you'll find that balance. That you'll get off this island and find your family."

20

What on Earth Are You Working For?

The time has come for me to reorganize my life, my peace—I cry out. I cannot adjust my life to secure any fruitful peace. Here I am at sixty-four, still seeking peace. It is a hopeless dream.
—H.G. WELLS

Pierre is a French Canadian whose story is well worth considering. A few years ago he was hiking near Montreal, Quebec, with a friend who was one of the wealthiest oil entrepreneurs in Canada. Stopping for a cool drink, Pierre asked his millionaire friend a question that had been troubling him for some time. "Why don't you invest more time in your family, in your children?"

Pierre's friend smiled, then said, "Pierre, don't you understand? I'm leaving them a legacy. Come, let me show you." Climbing a few hundred steps higher, the two reached a clearing in the woods and stopped. The entrepreneur stretched forth his hand and boasted, "See, I'm leaving this huge oil refinery. That's my legacy."

Two months later the wealthy oil baron died of a heart attack.

Less than a year later his company decided that the refinery no longer served its purposes. They dismantled and bulldozed it within days.

I come from a long line of storytellers. For decades, it's been one of the primary ways we have picked up truth around the Callaway household. My great-great-uncle on my father's side was a horse trader and perhaps the biggest liar ever to set foot on Canadian soil. In fact, I think he claimed to have discovered Canada when he got here. He liked to tell stories of how he invented the lightbulb and the printing press and green grass (it used to be blue, he said, like the stuff in Kentucky).

My father inherited this gift of storytelling, but thank goodness not the exaggerating. One night, after tucking me in, Dad sat on the side of my bed while the sunset faded to moonlight on my wall. He often told me stories, and this night was no exception. "There once was a man who wore red running shoes everywhere he went," he began. "Day after day, the man went racing through the streets of his village, frantically searching for something. Finally, a wise old preacher stopped him and asked, 'Why do you run so fast, and what are you looking for?'

"Out of breath, the man stopped, thought about it, and replied, 'I am chasing success.'

"The preacher laughed. 'Don't be silly,' he advised the runner. 'Success has been trying to catch up to you, but you are running too fast.'"

I still don't know why my dad told me this story or where it came from, for I was only six. But I have never forgotten it. Now, as I near middle age, the story comes back to ask me two questions: Why am I running so fast? And what am I missing as I run?

A pastor friend of mine told me this: "I am working so hard that my family has less of me. I do not enjoy life as I used to. My relationship with God is shallow, and I am tired most of the time."

When our world is on fast-forward we are like the man in the red shoes. Our motives are mangled, and we are moving at the speed of forgetfulness. We easily forget three things that I believe contribute to a successful life:

Time to Listen

An elderly couple enjoyed a rather opulent sixtieth wedding anniversary put on by their four children and many grandchildren. After the celebration, the husband saw his faithful companion of 60 years across the room. Though he loved her dearly, he remembered again how he had been concerned about her hearing problem lately. Since she was facing the other way, he thought he'd test her.

"Honey," he said from the other side of the room.

She didn't say anything, so he shuffled a few steps closer.

"Honey," he said again.

Still no response.

"Honey," he said a third time, "can you hear me?"

Again there was no reply. So he moved right behind her and whispered, "Honey."

At last she turned to him and said, "For the fourth time, what do you want?"

It's a long way to stretch a joke, but the story makes me think of my own hearing problem. So often I am moving too fast to listen. To my children. To my spouse. To my life.

Successful people somehow find time to listen. I am convinced that if you wore a T-shirt emblazoned with the words "I Listen," you'd be forced to balance things quickly, but you'd never be short of friends.

Time to Pray

This morning an e-mail advertisement informed me that we don't even need to take the time to pray anymore. Our computers will do it for us. "Your disk drive can now be turned into a prayer wheel," claims Deb Platt. On her Web page titled "Click Here for Good Karma," she boasts:

> To set your very own prayer wheel in motion, all you have to do is download this mantra to your computer's hard disk. Once downloaded, your hard disk drive will spin the mantra for you. Nowadays, hard disk drives spin their disks somewhere between 3600 and 7200 revolutions per minute, with a typical rate of 5400 rpm. Given those rotation speeds, you'll soon be purifying loads of negative karma.

If we click in all the right places, Deb assures us, our hard drives can serve as Mani wheels, spinning the mantra "Om Mani Padme Hum" (something parents yell at soccer games). Deb suggests that you can even enhance the "potency" of your hard drive prayer wheel by adding images of Tibetan Buddhist lamas or the Mahayana Buddhist teachings on compassion as the key to enlightenment. If you leave the computer on all night, she believes, the blessings will supersede even your power bill!

But if we are too busy to pray, aren't we simply too busy? Prayer leaves us alone with God. It forces us to remember that the world does not revolve around us, but around God Himself. Martin Luther said he had so much to do that he couldn't get along "without spending three hours daily in prayer." I have trouble relating to those words, but I must ask myself, "When was the last time in my busyness that I spent three *minutes* in prayer?" One of the sins that surely lies at the root of our busyness is the sin of prayerlessness. Jesus never taught His disciples how to preach or how to form multinational corporations, but He did teach them to pray. Leaving our requests at the feet of God changes us, bringing perspective and bringing peace.

Time to Give Thanks

A childhood friend of mine, now a missionary in Ethiopia, sent me the following:

If you have food in your fridge, clothes on your back, a roof over your head, and a bed to sleep in, you are richer than 75 percent of this world.

If you have money in the bank and spare change in a dish, you are among the top 8 percent of the world's wealthy.

If you woke up this morning with more health than sickness, you are more blessed than the million who will not survive the week.

If you have never experienced the danger of battle, the loneliness of imprisonment, or the pangs of starvation, you are ahead of 500 million people of the world.

If you can attend a church meeting without fear of harassment, arrest, torture, or death, you are more blessed than 3 billion people in the world.

If you hold up your head with a smile on your face and are truly thankful, you are blessed, because the majority can but most do not.

Take a few minutes this day and thank God for what you already have. If you are running too fast to listen, to pray, and to give thanks, you are running too fast.

In the midst of the busyness that characterizes our lives, we must take the time to listen. To pray. To thank those around us for the things they do. And to thank God for everything He's given us.

A successful life is a thankful life. A successful life is one that is poured into others.

21

The Telemarketing Cure

Somebody said to me, "But the Beatles were anti-materialistic." That's a huge myth. John and I literally used to sit down and say, "Now, let's write a swimming pool."
—PAUL MCCARTNEY

There are times when the telephone is a blessing. When it brings good news, a welcome voice, or some timely advice. But increasingly the phone brings a telemarketer—and often during the dinner hour. This was a problem for us until we got an answering machine. Now if there is an emergency—if, for instance, someone gets their tongue stuck on a flagpole in the winter—we are able to hear them scream through their cell phone and we go to the rescue. If they leave the correct address. Otherwise we continue our dinner-table conversation.

Sometimes I miss those chats with the telemarketers. It's important to remember that they are people too, and that they can be a lot of fun, particularly if you try the following:

Me: Hello?

AT&T: I'd like to speak to Mr. Callaway, please.

Me: Mr. Callaway is my dad. My name is Phil.

AT&T: Can I speak to your dad then?

Me: No, my wife won't let him live here.

AT&T: Um...Mr. Callaway, we would like to offer you 10 cents a minute, 7 days a week, 24 hours a day.

Me: WOW! THAT'S INCREDIBLE! HOW MUCH IS THAT? (with hand over receiver now) HONEY! WE WON!

AT&T: Pardon me?

Me: (rather excited) Let me go get a calculator. Just a second...

AT&T: Uh...Mr. Callaway—

Me: (pushing buttons on the calculator) Amazing! Ten cents a minute for a year is...let me see...$52,560. I won't even need to work anymore. Will you send me a check annually or once a month?

AT&T: Click.

The phone rang after dinner the other night. The caller was an acquaintance of mine, someone I hadn't seen since playing hockey against him in high school. It was good to hear his voice. "Phil," he began, "I just love your books. You really make me laugh."

I thanked him.

"Is it my picture on the back?" I asked.

He laughed again, then asked, "Do you have a minute?"

I did.

His voice suddenly turned businesslike. "Phil, I was just wondering if...well...could you see yourself making more money?"

There was silence and so he filled it.

"I have an excellent opportunity in sales and marketing. Could you see yourself taking more vacations? Having a nicer house? Being able to...well...to give more to needy people?"

I was shocked. Twenty-five years of silence broken by this?

I'M SORRY, MR. GRONEWALD, BUT RUNNING RED LIGHTS DOES NOT COUNT AS AN EXERCISE PROGRAM.

"No," I answered. "I'm very content right now. I have a good job. I spend time with my kids. I'm...well, very thankful."

There was more silence. It was his turn to be shocked.

"Uh...well...um...all the best there, Phil," he said. And hung up.

Perhaps the toughest response a telemarketer ever has to cope with is contentment.

Contentment is hardly a hallmark of our age. The Promised Land so many of us long for is one we will never see because it always exists in the future. Fleetwood Mac's song, "Don't stop thinking about tomorrow...It'll be better than before..." is our anthem. Our markets are about to expand, a new opportunity is on the horizon, our ship will come in (we hope we won't be at the bus stop when it does), the markets will rebound, we will strike it rich, we will hit the jackpot, we will uncover that pot of gold at the end of the rainbow.

Such thinking is always future tense. And I mean tense.

When we view life this way, today becomes an inconvenience. Today is a stepping-stone, a hurdle, a wall we must climb. Today we have to work long and hard to get to tomorrow. But when we reach tomorrow it becomes today, and the cycle returns. So we redouble our efforts, we work harder to succeed, we have miles to go before we sleep, and even then we may plug in a motivational tape to prompt our creative subconscious. One day we will be able to rest, we will lie down in green pastures, we will walk beside still waters, but not now. Now there is no time.

And so we put off living. We dream of some magical garden over the horizon, instead of enjoying the roses blooming outside our window today. But what if today is all we are given? What if we are never promised tomorrow? What then? What if we only have today to love and be loved? To celebrate friendship, to offer thanks, to take pleasure in life's simple wonders, impact others, and enjoy our work? What if the treasure we look for is hidden in the ground on which we stand?

My wife and I recently spent a lazy afternoon down by the oceanfront in Seattle, licking ice cream and strolling along the docks. The previous week had been jammed with activities, but the day was ours. The sun shone brightly—a rare occurrence in Seattle—so we ducked into the Pike Place Market. Suddenly we noticed a commotion. A crowd had gathered around a fish store—some with video cameras and most with wide smiles—to watch an unusual ritual take place. Now, if I asked how you'd like a job cutting up fish in a smelly fish store, you'd likely decline. Working with sharp knives, fish spines, and slimy scales is not something we wake up each morning hoping to do. Yet, here in the Pike Place Market, people were crowding around to watch creative employees actually enjoy a tedious job. They threw fish like footballs, they hollered loudly, they joked with customers. A string attached to one of the fish caused it to jump when a shopper came close, and the crowd grinned all the wider.

Fish has become the number one training film in the world. Its subject is how the managers of this Seattle fish market make cleaning, cutting up, and serving fish to customers a fun experience for everyone. The film has been a hit with people who work on factory assembly lines and x-ray your luggage at the airport. The employees are taught four simple principles when it comes to work:

1. Choose a positive attitude.

2. Play as you work.

3. Be there for the customer.

4. Make the customer's shopping day a memorable experience.

I'm sure the employees could spend their time thinking about tomorrow or the pot of gold Bill Gates has found a few miles away, but at the root of this philosophy is a simple word: contentment. We are content to squeeze the day. It may be a day blessed with sadness and joy, courage and fear, but with God's help we can make the best of it. As one of the workers at the fish market says, "You can start the day being either miserable or cheerful, so you might as well be cheerful."

A cheerful attitude comes from a spirit of contentment—not contentment with laziness or mediocrity, but a deep and abiding satisfaction that comes from doing the best we can with the tools we have. Our work is not drudgery, but something we are to take pleasure in today. Seattle's fish market is a contemporary reminder of the ancient words of the teacher in Ecclesiastes who taught us to take delight in our labor (2:24), and that it is a gift of God for us to be happy in our work (5:19).

Increasingly we live in a noisy, infringing culture. A culture that demands our attention. That delivers so much less than it promises. We call it the land of opportunity, but it is perhaps the land of importunity. The antidote is simplicity. The cure is contentment. The time to start is today.

I can think of no better way to conclude such thoughts, than to consider Jesus' liberating words in Matthew 6:31-34:

> So don't worry about having enough food or drink or clothing. Why be like the pagans who are so deeply concerned about these things? Your heavenly Father already knows all your needs, and he will give you all you need from day to day if you live for him...So don't worry about tomorrow, for tomorrow will bring its own worries. Today's trouble is enough for today (NLT).

22

The Last Stress Test

I like work; it fascinates me.
I can sit and look at it for hours.
—JEROME K. JEROME

There has never been a man in our history who led
a life of ease whose life is worth remembering.
—THEODORE ROOSEVELT

I enjoy putting up little signs around the office where I work. Some of them don't stay up long. Such as the one I taped to my boss's door just the other day: "The beatings will continue until the morale increases." But for the most part, my coworkers seem to appreciate a little humor. So I continue putting up such slogans as "Even though you're on the right track, you'll get run over if you just sit there."

On a list of most desirable traits to consider in hiring a new worker, a sense of humor ranks high. We all know that the workplace can use a little lightening up. A surveillance camera recently caught a frustrated employee slamming his fists on his keyboard and then looking up and punching his computer monitor until it crashed to the floor. Still angry, he jumped to his feet, marched around his desk, and began kicking the remains. Desk rage, office rage, and computer rage have entered our dictionaries alongside road rage, air rage, and outrage. Newspapers report an alarming increase in the number of employees in the workplace who shout,

I'VE CALLED THIS MEETING TO DISCUSS
THE PROBLEM OF STRESS IN THE WORKPLACE.

scream, threaten, gesture inappropriately, and sometimes commit physical assault.

Of course, not everyone experiences stress in the workplace. When I placed the following sign on the bulletin board, no one pulled it down. And I even caught a few people smiling at it: "In case of fire, flee building with the same reckless abandon that occurs each day at quitting time." Like these statements, the following quiz is designed to make you smile. It is also designed to help you assess where you are in achieving a balance between workaholism and sluggishness. Please take the following quiz with honesty. (Just don't take it too seriously.)

1. On your desk is the following plaque:

a. "If it's worth doing well, I'll have to do it."

b. "We the willing, led by the unknowing, are doing the impossible for the ungrateful. We have done so much for so long with so little we are now qualified to do anything with nothing."

c. "Lord, if you can't make me thin, make my friends look fat."

2. You believe Moses spent 40 years in the wilderness:

a. Selling mutual funds.

b. Because he had no cell phone.

c. Because he refused to ask his wife for directions.

3. Your idea of exercise is:

a. Twenty minutes on a StairMaster studying motivational books.

b. Bench-pressing the remote control.

c. Three-on-three basketball with friends.

4. Your hobbies consist of:

   a. Collecting frequent flyer points.

   b. Surfing the Net.

   c. Anything fun.

5. On your most recent vacation, you:

   a. Checked your answering machine eight times a day.

   b. Strolled sun-soaked beaches barefoot, basking in the glow of your spouse's eyes.

   c. Had to come home for a rest.

6. The thing you most like to bring with you when you golf is:

   a. A laptop computer.

   b. A cooler.

   c. Lots and lots of golf balls.

7. Your best friend drives up in a brand new Corvette. You:

   a. Place a tarp over your Chevy.

   b. Put a potato in his exhaust pipe.

   c. Say "Congratulations!"...and really mean it.

8. When it comes to ambition, your role model is:

   a. Bill Gates, who said, "Just in terms of allocation of time resources, religion is not very efficient. There's a lot more I could be doing on a Sunday morning."

   b. Bart Simpson.

   c. Jesus, who came to give His life away.

9. If you wrote down a brutally honest purpose statement it would go something like this:

a. I believe the fruit of the Spirit is push, shove, climb, race, and trample.

b. I hope to become a boss so I can get paid for watching other people work.

c. I believe there is a legitimate place for sweat and toil, but life is more than a climb to the top. Therefore, help me, Lord, to enjoy my work one day at a time, unhindered by my desire to get ahead.

10. Your life verse is:

a. Hezekiah 3:16: "A man's life consists of the abundance of his *positions*."

b. 1 Corinthians 9:27: "I *buffet* my body..." something you love to do at fine restaurants everywhere.

c. Colossians 3:23: "Whatever you do, work at it with all your heart, as working for the Lord, not for men."

How to score: If you answered "a" more than six times, thank you for taking this quiz while riding your treadmill. Please take another aspirin and continue reading this book. If you found yourself gravitating to the "b" responses, kindly peel yourself from the couch and check your pulse. Call a doctor if necessary. If you chose "c" five or more times, congratulate yourself. And hang up the following slogan in the office: "To make a long story short, there's nothing like having the boss walk in."

23

The Road to Happiness

If only God would give me some clear sign—like making a large deposit in my name at a Swiss bank.
—Woody Allen

You'll be glad to know that, contrary to what your mother told you, money can now buy you happiness. A team of British economists says so. After studying 10,000 people in Britain during the last decade, Jonathan Gardner and Andrew Oswald of Warwick University have placed the price of happiness at 2 million. "It would take a lottery win or other cash boost of similar size to lift people out of misery," they claim. "If somebody started off being miserable relative to the rest of the population, 2 million would be enough to make them more cheerful than most others," says the report.

Ever since I was a kid I have been told that money can't buy happiness, but I sure wanted a chance to find out for myself. "Money won't buy happiness," said comedian Bill Vaughan, "but it will pay the salaries of a huge research staff to study the problem."

I haven't studied 10,000 people myself, but a lifetime of living and observing gives me cause to question the economists' findings. My dad once asked my mother if she would like to open a joint savings account with him, and she declined. Said she preferred to open one with someone who had money. I think Dad took a low-paying job so he wouldn't lose much if he was fired. I'm kidding of course, but although my parents were paupers in the area of money, they were princes in the realm of happiness. You don't need the glitter to have the glow.

Dr. Shaun Saunders of the University of Newcastle in South Wales recently told participants at the European Congress of Psychology conference in London, "It has always been said that money can't buy you happiness. We have measured it scientifically—and found that it is absolutely true."

A team quizzed 1400 people aged 18 to 60 on their attitude toward possessions and levels of satisfaction with life. "The more materialistic people were, the more depressed they tended to be," observed Dr. Saunders. "In our society, the criterion tends to be what you own. The problem is that if you feel that your sense of worth or value is tied up in what you own, then the things you own are not likely to hold their value for very long. In our market-driven society, things are very often yesterday's fashions or not worth what they were. If you determine your personal worth from possessions—things that are outside yourself—then you are setting yourself up for a very big fall."

The life of Dawn Wilby seems to support these findings. The 31-year-old from Barnsley, England, won more than $8 million in the national lottery recently. A miner's daughter, Dawn lived in rented accommodations and worked as a clerk. After the windfall, she quit her job and bought a $320,000 detached home and a Volkswagen Golf convertible. But happiness proved illusory. Ten months later she took a job with financial consultants for $25,000, saying she had been "as miserable as sin" staying in bed late, watching television in the afternoon, and hitting the town at night.

In the ancient wisdom masterpiece Ecclesiastes, the teacher writes, "Those who love money will never have enough. How absurd to think that wealth brings true happiness! The more you have, the more people come to help you spend it" (Ecclesiastes 5:10-11 NLT). The writer then turns the coin over and examines the other side: "It is a good thing to receive wealth from God and the good health to enjoy it. To enjoy your work and accept your lot in life— that is indeed a gift from God. People who do this rarely look with sorrow on the past, for God has given them reasons for joy" (Ecclesiastes 5:19-20 NLT).

Invest in Others

Before his recent death, I had the chance to spend an hour with billionaire Robert Van Kampen, pioneer of the insured mutual fund. At the time he was managing six companies with investments of nearly $80 billion—slightly more than my weekly allowance when I was a child. Quick to laugh even as he struggled with a heart condition, Mr. Van Kampen talked of the joy of giving. "What makes my life rich is giving money away," he said.

"I'm here to make you rich," I joked.

But he was serious. "I've found that you can never outgive God," he said, glancing at a small gadget that monitored his heart. "If you give to get, chances are you won't get a dime. If you're giving out of a heart of gratitude for what God has given you, God turns around and blesses you. I've made some huge errors," he said, shaking his head. "I've lost more money in a year than some countries make. But the Lord makes it up to you if your motive is right...I started with nothing, and I've been incredibly successful. God has trusted me with these funds, and He could take them away at any moment. God rewards faithfulness whether we have a little or a lot."

Want What You Have

I just spent an evening with a couple who earn approximately three times what my wife and I earn, but they spent much of the time complaining about debts they had accumulated and the rising cost of living. They smiled when I explained how we are able to live on one income, and then they went back to complaining about money and how their children must have the latest toys and designer clothes.

Before I left, they asked me for a loan.

The average home in Ridgewood, New Jersey, is worth $457,000. Many residents were killed in the Trade Center attack on September 11, and those who mourned the dead are also mourning a lifestyle, says Ivan Scibberas, a local pastor. Following the attacks, he heard from the wives whose husbands left for work on Wall Street at 5 a.m. about the cost of all this striving. "I am not deceived at all by seeing these beautiful homes," he told Alanna Mitchell of the *Globe and Mail.* "Never have I met as much sadness...Long before September 11 they were questioning whether the large homes and three BMWs they had were enough [to satisfy]."

When the twin towers in New York fell, it was the final crushing blow for some. They felt as though they had lived their lives deceived. Sciberras says that when police came looking for information about what the missing had been wearing, most of the wives didn't know. They hadn't been awake when their husbands had left for work. "So many people are mourning," says Sciberras. "They see that this kind of lifestyle that has promised them so much somehow fails to deliver."

As surely as a car will not run on sugar, the human soul was not meant to thrive on stuff. We were made for more than this.

Yet when we turn our backs on this truth, we try all the harder.

A letter that arrived on my desk just this afternoon outlines the frustration of a college student.

> Life at home is tougher than dorm life because of the selfishness. We have more things in our house than we have places for them. But every word out of my mother's mouth has to do with not having enough money. We are so miserable talking about

what we don't have that we rarely glance at the
things we do have. I don't want anything from
my parents except their love. And I hope they'll
stay together.

If you want to influence others, if you want a great return
on your investment, invest in contentment. "Godliness with
contentment," says the apostle Paul in 1 Timothy 6:6, "is
great gain."

Discover the Missing Peace

Recently while on an airplane, I read a full-page ad in the
newspaper. The bold headline proclaimed: "Wealthy Man
Wants to Give You His Wealth Secret Before It's Too Late!"

I was intrigued. The millionaire's name is John Wright, and
he boasts four homes, a Rolls Royce, a Mercedes, a million-
dollar line of credit at the bank, and much more—happiness
and peace of mind.

"Imagine how your whole life will change if you use this
secret to get all the money you need," says John. "You won't
have to worry about bills. Nobody will boss you around.
You will have more time to spend with your loved ones. You
can have the house you want, the car you want, the vacations
you want. And best of all, you will finally have PEACE OF
MIND!"

All of this for only $58.

Isaiah 26:3 tells us where we will find lasting peace of
mind, and it won't even cost you $58. "You will keep in per-
fect peace all who trust in you [God], whose thoughts are
fixed on you!" (NLT).

Like Martin Buber's story of Rabbi Eisik who went
searching from city to city for treasure only to discover that
the greatest treasure was under his stove back home, many
realize too late that happiness is the one thing you can't chase
down. You have to let it catch you.

True and lasting happiness does not come from the treasures found "out there." The possessions, the beauty, the

fame, or the winning personality. Yes, some possess these things and are happy. But there is no necessary correlation. In a culture that equates happiness with material things, outward beauty, and personality traits, we need to be reminded that happiness cannot be had in the searching, but in the resting. The red SUV or the stucco home or the Caribbean cruise will not make our lives complete. The weekend seminar and books such as *Ten Easy Steps to Happiness* or *Seven Ways to Be Thin by Next Tuesday* do not lead to peace. We seek treasure out there somewhere, in another city—when the real treasure is under our stove at home.

I didn't pay attention enough in school, but 40 years of living have taught me this much: Those who chase happiness run away from contentment, so don't pursue what is illusory. Nothing should be done in haste except swatting mosquitoes. Property and position and prestige can be had, but they usually cost you your nerves. Live with an open hand and a thankful heart. Don't confuse success with fruitfulness. Keep your soul free from hate and your mind from worry. Envy of others eats you alive, so celebrate with them when they succeed. And be silent when they do not. Be content. Do not fear misfortune. Live life simply. Expect little. Give much. Purify your heart and love your God. And cherish above all else those who love you enough to do your laundry.

24

Changing Currency

Life is short and we never have too much time for gladdening the hearts of those who are traveling the dark journey with us. Oh be swift to love, make haste to be kind.

—Henri Frederick Amiel

Twice a week I enjoy lunch in a popular submarine sandwich shop a block from my office. The custom began with a trip to the doctor. He squinted and tapped and prodded and probed, then typed into his computer and looked at me with a deep furrow in his brow. "So, Phil," he said, "how much exercise do you get?"

"Those are pretty funny posters on your wall, Doc," I said.

"I'm serious, Phil."

"Well...uh...I walk to work sometimes, I push buttons on a remote, I...uh...I avoid deadlines."

He was neither impressed nor humored. "How soon do you want to die, Phil? You're doing too much too fast without a retreat. You're running on fumes. You need more exercise than just running from deadline to deadline."

"But I'm not an exercise kind of guy," I said defensively. "I love sports, but I don't like to know that I'm exercising when I do them. I don't run around tracks or walk on treadmills. It seems like mindless gerbil activity to me."

"It's not, Phil," he said.

I told the doctor that I had some problems with the basic philosophy of exercise. "Financially, it's a bad decision," I explained. "For every minute you exercise, you add one minute to your life. In the end you could end up spending an additional five months in a nursing home at $5000 a month."

He didn't even smile.

"The only advantage of exercise," I suggested, "is that you die healthier. My motto is 'No pain, no pain.'"

He didn't laugh at all.

"My own mother started walking a mile a day when she was 60," I said, a little louder. "She's 78 now, and we can't find her."

His face broke into a grin, and he laughed out loud.

"Do you eat well?" he asked, after clearing his throat and composing himself.

"Very well, thank you," I said. "I eat foods fried in vegetable oil, so I get my vegetables. I eat lots of red meat because cows eat hay and corn. Beef is a great source of green leafy field grass."

"You should be a comedian," said the doctor. "But you may not live long enough. Do something, Phil. I don't want your wife to be a widow just yet."

Over the next few days I thought about his wisdom, then finally called my friend James. "I'll buy you lunch tomorrow if you go to the aquatic center with me first," I told him. He agreed. And so began a tradition that has grown more enjoyable with each passing week. For 20 minutes James swims. Because I swim with all the grace of a half-ton truck, I ride the stair machine nearby, reading things I have to read anyway. Afterwards we get together and discuss which parts of our bodies hurt and how badly.

The beauty of the digital readouts on these newfangled machines is that you can tell how many calories you've shed

I CAN'T TALK TO YOU NOW, MOTHER.
YOU KNOW THIS IS MY BUSIEST DAY OF THE YEAR!

in 20 minutes. Today, for instance, I used up 281 calories, so I had to replace them with something. I chose a submarine sandwich, a soda, and a small chocolate bar (okay, it was a large one).

Exercise is a good thing, but better yet, these lunches have been the start of a fabulous and sacred friendship that I wouldn't trade for all the chocolate in Hershey, Pennsylvania.

On the other three days of my working week, I experience another joy of small-town living—the simple pleasure of lunch at home. Most days I walk, taking perhaps five or six minutes to get there, then I sit on the back porch with my wife, munching sandwiches, surveying the ripening wheat fields, or just talking about our children who are stuck at school.

The time is ours.

One day when I walked past my son's school with lunch on my mind, his class was hitting golf balls into a field under the watchful gaze of the physical education instructor. The instructor, a friend of mine, called me over and challenged me to a duel with one of the students. Whoever hit a ball closest to an orange cone would be the recipient of a soda at the other's expense. He handed me a club that Noah used on the Ark.

I swung the club. And lost. Badly.

Walking home with my head down I thought of some good excuses. I hadn't stretched. The club was old. *I* am old. Then came an idea. It would cost me ten dollars, delay lunch, and leave a few things undone. But as I walked, I wondered how many more years my son would be standing among his classmates, a shy grin on his face, watching his dad make a fool of himself, and perhaps feeling just a little bit proud of him for doing so.

Grabbing my wallet, I jumped in our van and drove to the grocery store. Half an hour later I pulled cans from a cooler full of ice and watched a class of 23 gulp a 24-pack of soda in record time. "Thanks, Mr. Callaway," they kept saying. "That was cool."

Sometimes our children will remember the big things—the trip to Disneyland or a plane ride to another time zone. I think Stephen will remember the time he was glad a class-mate beat his dad.

One of the greatest tragedies of a fast-forward world is that we are less available to be surprised by the sponta-neous. As we sacrifice relationships on the altar of busyness, we come to the end of the day tired but unfulfilled. All day we made ourselves unavailable for a kind word, a game of chess, the sound of a child's laughter, the smell of fresh bread baking. Like the African farmer who sold his farm to search for diamonds, not knowing that his property would turn into one of the largest diamond mines in all of Africa, we forget that the greatest treasures on earth are sometimes found in our own backyard. But we may not have tomorrow to hold those treasures close and to celebrate the joy they bring.

I had a startling reminder of this last winter when I took my daughter, Rachael, to the swimming pool one evening. It was 20 below zero outside, so we ended up sitting in the hot tub surrounded by small children and adults—some who looked like rather well-done lobsters.

"Dad," said Rachael, tugging on my arm, "can I have two dollars for some treats?"

"Nope," I said.

"Well, can we go out for ice cream after?"

I told her we couldn't, that we had better get home, that it was cold outside, that I had miles to go before I slept.

The man beside me, a complete stranger, looked my way and whispered, "You take her. If you need the money, I'll give it to you." Turning, I noticed that there were tears in his eyes. "I'd give just about anything to take my daughter out for ice cream tonight," he said, so quietly I had to strain to hear him. "She...she died of leukemia three years ago."

"I'm so sorry," I said.

That night we enjoyed ice cream together, Rachael and I, across the street from the submarine shop. I extracted slow licks from a single scoop of vanilla. She decided on double scoops—Bubble Gum Rainbow and Peanut Butter. We bowed our heads in the little coffee shop. I prayed for the man who had lost his daughter, gave quiet thanks for life's small blessings, and sat there wondering what would happen if we changed currencies. If we began measuring wealth in terms of friendship and time and life's small pleasures.

"Did you know that I'm a millionaire?" I asked my daughter, when we lifted our heads. Her eyes widened, she gulped, and almost lost her ice cream cone to the floor.

"Really?" she asked rather excitedly.

"Really," I said. "You see, this time with you right now is worth about $10,000 to me. Lunch with Mom is worth the same. We're rich, Rachael. Rich in memories, rich in relationships, rich in laughter."

"So," she said, looking past peanut butter ice cream, "if we're so rich, can I have the two dollars for treats?"

25

Rat-Race Living

*If you are miserable or bored in your work...or
dread going to it...then God is speaking to you. He
either wants you to change the job you are in—or
more likely, he wants to change you.*
—BRUCE LARSON

Martha Bolton is one of the funniest people I've had the
pleasure of meeting. She writes serious theological treatises
such as *Honey, the Carpet Needs Weeding*. For many years
she wrote jokes for comedian Bob Hope. Martha and I keep
in touch, mostly via e-mail. The other day she sent me this,
which is from her book *Still the One* (Revell):

You know you're a workaholic if...

- you use Maalox as gravy.

- you consider a walk to Kinko's your evening exercise.

- your home movies have the Wall Street report crawling
  across the bottom of the screen.

- your laptop has seen more of your lap than your children have.

- while being wheeled into the emergency room, you
  hand a file to the nurse and say, "Here, fax this."

- you use digital technology to add your image to family pictures.

- the last time you stopped and smelled the roses was when you fell asleep at the wheel and crashed into a flower shop.

- you play lullabies to your children using the tones on your cell phone and beeper.

- you've been known to use your computer mouse pad as a pillow.

- while showing off your new baby's hospital picture to some friends, your wife reminds you that he just turned 17!

Here are a few other wise suggestions from friends of mine.

> At 36 I was informed by my doctor that an innocent little lump was full of cancer cells. With months of chemotherapy ahead of me, I found that work fell fast down my list of priorities. I began taking long walks in the evenings and looking more at the sky than the ground. I took up bird-watching. I just celebrated my thirty-eighth birthday surrounded by more friends than I've ever had in my life. I'm more inclined to tell them I love them now. I work with people who send me home when I look tired. I make less money than before, and I give more away. I do more walking and looking. I pick more daisies.
> —SARAH HANSON

Last summer after 15 years of missionary life in Bolivia, we uprooted and moved to Miami,

Florida. We considered ourselves busy on the mission field, but the pace of life in this megacity of 4 million has many times come close to overwhelming us. Long commutes. Traffic jams. Constant noise. The bureaucracy of setting up a house, furnishings, utilities, and vehicles with their corresponding licenses as well as enrolling children in the Florida health and education system (this country's most regulation-laden) all proved far more complex than we expected. And I mustn't forget that time-eating American cultural aberration to which we have been introduced—telemarketing at every hour of the day and evening. Add full-time jobs, church, school, and ministry activities, and we are beginning to wonder how our friends here managed to keep sane all these years. Life in Latin America is event-oriented. An activity or social event starts when it starts, and then one enjoys it until it is over. America is time-oriented. One is continually watching the clock and rushing to the next activity before taking time to enjoy and assimilate the last. Great for productivity, but not so for stress.

—JEANETTE WINDLE

My wife has had some serious health problems, and I am pastoring a tiny Baptist church. But even though the church is small, there always seems to be more to do than there is time for. Last year was a bad year. Pretty well every day was stressful. I had to remind myself that "the need is not the call," and I cut back my involvement in a couple of things. As a result, this year has been a great improvement.

—BOB COTTRILL

WHAT DO YOU MEAN I'VE GOT AN ULCER?
I DON'T _GET_ ULCERS - - I _GIVE_ THEM !

I have chosen cash over plastic. You see, I once found it too easy to whip out the credit card and move on to the next store. And then the bill would come and I would repent, starting the whole cycle over again. The benefit of cash is that I have started being more careful with what I buy. Having cash has made me stop and question whether I really need that stainless steel egg flipper when it might mean that my children go without apples for a week. I know in advance what I have to spend, so I have learned to wait for stuff. And often, in the waiting, I forget about the very thing I thought I had to have at that moment.

—CAROLYNE AARSEN

I have started measuring my wealth not by what I possess, but by what I am able to give away. Some native cultures don't know anything about potlucks, but they do celebrate *potlatch,* or the great giveaway, when gifts are freely given to others in the community. They do not give away junk, but the finest of what they have. If I can afford to give away the best that I have, and do so without thought of reward or fanfare, I am very rich indeed.

—TONY LINDELL

PART FOUR

The Fruit of the Spirit Is Not Lemons

*With the fearful strain that is on me day and night,
if I did not laugh, I should die.*

—ABRAHAM LINCOLN

*But the fruit of the Spirit is love, joy, peace,
patience, kindness, goodness, faithfulness,
gentleness and self-control. Against such things
there is no law.*

—GALATIANS 5:22-23

26

Laughing Matters

*Life need not be easy to be joyful. Joy is not the
absence of trouble, but the presence of Christ.*
—WILLIAM VANDER HOVEN

On Sunday afternoon I usually manage to make it to the
couch shortly after the dishes are done, but today I didn't
quite make it. Today I hit the floor in the living room and
drifted off to sleep within seconds. My children saw me
there, a rather large and inviting target, I suppose, because
the three of them pounced upon me as I slept. I'm sure it
was funny for them, but I happened to be dreaming at the
time. In my dream two KGB officers, who suspected me of
concealing military secrets in my trench coat, were pursuing
me on foot through the darkened back alleys of our small
town. They cornered me by a garden shed, pinning me by
the arms. I tried to wiggle. I could not. Waking, I found a
child sitting on one of those arms, another on the other,
and the third on his way to the pantry to get a Cheerio.
Pulling my shirt up, he inserted the piece of cereal in my
belly button. "Here, Mojo!" he yelled, and the dog came
running.

Pointing to the Cheerio, he hollered, "Get it, get it, get it!"

You have choices at such a time. Not many of them. But
there are a few. I chose to join in. "Whatever you do," I said,

between gasps of painful laughter, "don't put honey on my forehead."

You know what happened next.

They even dabbed it on my lips. Children make us cry sometimes, but more often they help us laugh.

My son Jeffrey has a contagious laugh, one that spills out of his room, down the street, and even into the church. When he was very small, he started screaming during a sermon, so I grabbed him and whisked him out the back. As I pushed open the doors he yelled over my shoulder, "Pray for me!"

He's been making us laugh ever since.

I am convinced that few things are more important than a good sense of humor in leading a balanced, joy-filled, peaceful life in a fast-forward world.

Laughter, stress, and worry cannot coexist for long. Stress inflates our balloons to the popping point; laughter slowly releases the pressure. Laughter is cholesterol-free and contains no MSG, no fat grams, and no negative side effects. Although it got me into a ton of trouble in fifth grade, laughter never committed a crime or started a war, and there is no record of anyone who died laughing. It has finished many an argument, however. I have seen laughter disarm, revive, motivate, encourage, and cheer. Laughter is the shortest distance between two people, and it is one of the few things the government still doesn't tax!

But laughter is not always easy to come by. Life is difficult. Times are tough.

While speaking at a minister's retreat, I noticed one couple sitting in the front row at each of my sessions (speakers don't forget such things). The wife was a brilliant and witty woman who laughed at all of my jokes, but her husband sat there glaring at me. For three days, I tried to make him laugh. Nothing worked. He was so sour he looked as if he could suck buttons off a sofa. After the final session, his wife approached me with a smile and an extended hand. "I just

MY HUSBAND BELIEVES THAT LAUGHTER SHOULD BE
RESERVED FOR STRICTLY MEDICINAL PURPOSES.

want to thank you," she said. "I haven't seen my husband laugh this hard in years." Unfortunately, I meet such people with increasing frequency. Life's difficulties have them pinned to the mat; the speed of life has them cornered. But it needn't be.

My wife's sister, Miriam, suffers from Huntington's disease, a rare genetic disorder that causes rapid mental and physical deterioration. Doctors who treat thousands of Huntington's patients are amazed at how slowly this awful disease is growing in Miriam's body. The reasons are numerous—a loving husband and family, a positive attitude that never ceases to amaze us, and perhaps most noticeably, an easy laugh. Those who have every reason to cry and yet choose to laugh seem to have a jump start on life. "Miriam's attitude," a doctor told her husband, Jim, "has reduced the symptoms of Huntington's by 50 percent."

"It seems that your belief in a higher power has helped you," a psychologist said to Miriam and her husband one day.

Miriam smiled. "That would be God," she said.

Hers is the laughter of one who has discovered the fine art of living: enjoying what we can see and not complaining about what remains in the dark. Life may be falling apart at the edges, but not at the core. At the very center, Miriam knows that she is loved by God, held in His arms, and that He has promised to her the eternal joys of heaven. She has learned that God gives us enough light for the next step, so she rejoices in the little light she's given, not asking for a great spotlight to take all the shadows away.

For Miriam, laughter has plugged the springs of bitterness, put a permanent cork on tension, and soothed the crippling pain of disappointment.

In the midst of my personal burnout, I spent some time with Ken Davis, an internationally renowned comedian and one of the funniest men I know. I told him what I was experiencing and how much of the joy and laughter had vacated my life. Our conversation became a healthy dialogue on our real reason to laugh.

"We Christians have every reason to laugh," Ken told me, "because the most serious issues were dealt with when Jesus died on the cross. Death lost its sting, and we are free to discover those things in life around us that carry unbelievable gems of joy, and to throw back our heads and laugh. The apostle Paul said, 'For me to live is Christ, and to die is gain.' That kind of person is free. Real laughter comes from a deep sense of joy. It's possible to laugh without joy, but I find it very difficult to believe that a person who has joy doesn't laugh."

Much of Ken's humor has grown from adversity. For one thing, he can't turn his arms a certain way—something I noticed when we first golfed together. It gives Ken an excuse if I beat him. Ken grew up in a somewhat crippling, legalistic environment. "There wasn't much laughter in our home," he recalls. "There were times when we had fun, but there was also a lot of tension. I grew up in a very strict home, and there was a time when I rebelled and went exactly the opposite way."

Ken has motivated millions the world over with his sense of humor, and he doesn't get too many complaints. But occasionally someone will say, "How can you talk about Jesus one minute and laugh the next?" His response: "How can I not? Because of what Christ has done, I'm free to laugh." "I don't get a lot of negative feedback," laughs Ken, "because when anyone comes toward me with something other than a smile on their face, I run!"

One of the greatest reasons for joy, Ken believes, is that we are not some accident of slimy algae, as too many are being taught in school, but the purposeful creation of a magnificent God. "Before the foundation of the world, God had our picture on His wall," Ken smiles. "This same God who gave us a hilarious world and who created us unique and wonderful, chose to give His Son that we might live. He loves us and proved it with His gift of Christ. That is our ultimate reason for joy and peace. That joy stays when you can't laugh anymore. When you are burned out or in the midst of tragedy. That joy is there when you have sinned and desperately need forgiveness. That joy never goes away."

27

The Parrot Trap

A day of worry is more exhausting
than a day of work.
—SIR JOHN LUBBOCK (1834–1913)

I once talked with a doctor who made an interesting claim: "Seventy percent of all the patients who come to me," he said, "could cure themselves if they would just get rid of their worry and fear."

Without a doubt one of the greatest stress inducers is worry. I should know. I took up worrying in fifth grade. At Bible camp that summer, I kissed a girl named Patty Gilbert as she worked on a leathercraft. I even asked her to marry me, but she said her boyfriend would kill me if she did. And so I began worrying that he would come looking for me. Small things have big shadows when you worry—especially after dark.

I learned to worry about everything. My parents went on a trip, and I worried that they wouldn't come back. And then I worried that if they did return, they'd find out what I'd done while they were gone. It is a never-ending and vicious cycle, this worrying. And if you are a worrywart, the onset of years only brings more things to worry about. You go from worrying about diapers to worrying about diplomas. From worrying about getting a job to keeping one. And in

HONEY, THIS IS LARRY AND JULIE, THEY ARE YOUNG WORRIEDS.

the end, you worry about whether or not the wheels on your shopping cart will all go in the same direction.

All my life I've had to fight worry. Like pesky mosquitoes, those small worries sap our energy and send us in, out of the bright sunshine. Perhaps the only good thing about worrying is that the things we worry about never seem to happen.

In my experience, more people are addicted to worry than all the other addictions combined. And if anything drains the joy from life with gusto, it is worry.

Worry is like an exercise bicycle—it gives you something to do but it doesn't really take you anywhere. Worry forces us to live life focusing on the nonessentials, squinting at the unknown. You don't notice the blessings around you when you worry. And you miss out on the most important things in life. This fact is illustrated perfectly by a story I've told my kids a dozen times over the years. I hope you enjoy it as much as they do.

The loneliest lady in town sat in her house year after lonely year with the shades drawn and the curtains pulled. Finally, she decided to do something to conquer her loneliness.

Dropping by Henry's Pet Store, she looked over her options. There were dogs and cats and guppies and gerbils— even snakes. She hated snakes. And the other animals didn't seem quite right. "I need a pet that will be a good companion," she told the store owner Henry, who was bald as a billiard ball. "I need a pet that is almost like having another human around the house."

"Aha," said Henry, "I have just the thing." Motioning her to the back of the store, he pulled a flowered blanket off a large birdcage and pointed out the perfect pet—a colorful parrot.

"Does it talk?" asked the customer.

"Absolutely...a real chatterbox," replied the owner. "You'll be amazed at its friendly disposition and wide vocabulary. It can even say anthropomorphic. That's why it's so expensive."

The lonely lady winced at the price tag, but she bought the parrot and brought it home in a large silver cage. At last she had the perfect companion. One she could talk to. One who would answer back.

But the first week passed without the bird saying a single thing. Beginning to worry, the lonely lady walked to the pet shop for advice.

"How's that parrot?" asked Henry. "Quite a talker, eh?"

"No," replied the woman. "He hasn't said one word since I bought him. I'm worried."

"Well," said Henry, scratching his bald head, "did you buy a mirror when you bought the bird?"

The lady hadn't thought of that.

"There's your problem. When a parrot looks at itself, it begins to chatter."

So she bought the mirror, placed it in the cage, and began talking to the bird for hours on end. The parrot only stared at her in silence. Now she was really worried.

"The bird isn't talking at all," she told Henry a week later. "I've tried everything."

"Did you buy a ladder when you got the cage?"

"No," replied the lady. "Will that make it talk?"

"Works every time," Henry replied. "The parrot looks in the mirror and gets a little exercise on the ladder. Before long you won't be able to stop all the chatter."

So she purchased the ladder and placed it in the cage. Still nothing. She would lie awake at night worrying about the bird. Why won't it talk? What can I do?

"Did you buy a swing?" Henry asked her the next week. "The parrot looks at himself, takes a stroll up and down the ladder, then relaxes on the swing. Before long—bingo! Anthropomorphic. He's talking."

So she bought the swing, brought it home, and placed it in the cage. Still not a word from the parrot.

A week later she came bursting into the pet store. The owner met her at the counter. "Hey, how's the—"

"It's dead! My expensive bird is dead in the bottom of the cage!"

"I'm so sorry. Did it ever say anything at all?"

"Yes," replied the lady. "Just before it died, it said, 'Isn't there anything to eat around here?'"

Few things waste more time and energy than worry. It causes us to focus on the wrong things, to live our lives facing the wrong direction.

Winning Over Worry

My own burnout was partly worry induced. In the wake of it all, I began reading books. Believe it or not, I read three or four Hardy Boys mystery books, a favorite activity when I was sick as a child. But a far more helpful activity was the immersing of myself in the New Testament book of Philippians. Tucked away in its last chapter, I found what I'd been missing—a guaranteed cure for worrywarts. Read it carefully:

> Don't worry about anything; instead, pray about everything. Tell God what you need, and thank him for all he has done. If you do this, you will experience God's peace, which is far more wonderful than the human mind can understand. His peace will guard your hearts and minds as you live in Christ Jesus...Fix your thoughts on what is true and honorable and right. Think about things that are pure and lovely and admirable...things that are excellent and worthy of praise...and the God of peace will be with you (Philippians 4:6-9 NLT).

Many of us live by the slogan "Why pray when you can worry?" We must reverse the slogan. When something we cannot control or change frightens and agitates us, we should emblazon "You can worry or you can pray" across a mirror, a dashboard, or a birdcage.

Feeding your mind with positive thoughts can be the difference between depression and joy. Whatever is pure and lovely and admirable probably won't make for high ratings on prime time. But focusing on these things will change our outlook.

What are you feeding your mind?

George MacDonald once wrote, "No man ever sank under the burden of the day. It is when tomorrow's burden is added to the burden of today that the weight is more than a man can bear. Never load yourself so."

The happiest people I know are those who have learned to hold loosely the things of earth and have handed the worrisome, stress-filled details of their daily lives into God's keeping.

Worry is a no-confidence vote in God. Let your worry be replaced by simple trust in Him. He is at work. He is in control. He is in the middle of whatever is happening, has happened, or will happen. And He will never take His children where He has not been.

Remember, you don't need to put your umbrella up until it rains. So starve your worries—but feed your pets.

28

The Last Gift

*The grace of God is in my mind
shaped like a key, that comes from time to time
and unlocks the heavy doors.*
—Donald Swan

The older I get, the more I'm convinced that memory and smell are linked. I close my eyes and I can almost smell Christmas. Sugar cookies baking. The turkey sizzling. I love the taste of Christmas. Mixed nuts. Mandarin oranges. Fresh dirt from one of my brother Tim's incoming snowballs. Ah, Christmastime.

When I was a child of eight or nine and Christmas was barely a week away, I sinned greatly. I sneaked into Grandpa's room, listened to him snore, then reached out and stole an entire box of chocolates, locking myself in the bathroom and eating both layers. I can still taste those chocolates. I can still feel that strap. Few sins were worth the spankings. This one came close. It made me wonder if sometimes you're almost better off asking for forgiveness than permission.

Each December morning my sister and I would sit on a living room heat register inches from the Christmas tree, coveting toys from the Sears catalog. On the wall behind our heads, white frost had crept through the openings of an electrical outlet. Yesterday I'd earned a nickel putting my tongue on it. But otherwise I was a reasonably bright chap. The earth was somehow colder in those primitive days. Snowdrifts were higher. Winter was longer. As we sat on the heat vent, my sister pointed out certain toys in the catalog. "What do they do?" she asked. If I didn't know the answer, I made one up. "This doll's head wobbles side to side," I'd say. "Then it pops off." My sister was impressed with my knowledge.

One page in particular held a dream for me. At the top right, just above a stuffed orange bear, sat a yellow-handled bow with real suction cup arrows. "If only I could pull the wrapping off one of those," I told my sister, "my Christmas would be complete." She shook her head. "Impossible," she said. "There's no money." And when I told my brother, he agreed with my sister. "You kidding?" he laughed. "After what you did to Grandpa's chocolates? You'll be lucky to get a hand-me-down toothbrush."

Deep down I knew he was right. Deep down I dreaded Christmas. But still I shared the dream with my dad. "Ten dollars and ninety-nine cents," he winced. "You want to put us in the Poor House?" I wondered what the Poor House was like. What would we do there? Would Grandpa still come visit? Would he bring chocolates?

As December 25 drew near, I scanned the growing pile beneath the tree. Nothing. A shiny green package near the back was the right size, but late one night while everyone else slept, a flashlight informed me that the name tag was my sister's. In fact, most of them seemed to be hers. I squeezed the ones that said "Philip." They felt like practical gifts—socks, deodorant, underwear. Things you don't tell your friends about on Boxing Day.

The worst thing about Christmas morning was the waiting. My parents made us eat breakfast first. Then do the dishes. And sweep floors. And vacuum carpets. And memorize the Gospel of Luke. Then Dad prayed for the troops in Vietnam and Korea and Russia, and missionaries in countries I couldn't pronounce.

At last the time came. And this year the disappointment was overwhelming. With only three presents left beneath the tree, I held in my lap a small Tonka truck, three pairs of black socks, a shirt with pins in it, and a cowboy poster that read "When you reach the end of your rope, tie a knot in it and hang on."

The first remaining gift was a George Beverly Shea record album for my mom. The second was for Grandpa, a box of chocolates from my brother and me. The last gift was green and shiny and just the right size. My sister grinned. And picked it up. Then the most unexpected thing happened: She turned and handed it to me. "Open it," she said. "It's yours. Tim put my name on it to fool you."

Mom wanted me to save the wrapping paper for next year, but it was already too late. I let out a triumphant *"Whoop!"* and danced around the living room, holding the bow and arrow high like the Stanley Cup. Grandpa stopped sampling chocolates and smiled widely. "It's from all of us," he said.

"You be careful with that, son," said my mother.

"He'll be okay," said my dad.

I remember only a handful of gifts from my childhood. A Detroit Red Wings hockey jersey. A Hot Wheels race car set. I remember ice-skating and carol singing and candle making, and Grandpa's story of a Baby whose tiny brow was made for thorns; whose blood would one day cleanse the world.

But it was the last gift that made Christmas come alive for me.

You see, that bow and arrow caused me to realize that Christmas is all about grace. A gift I don't deserve, coming along when I least expect it. Changing everything. Forever. "For to us a child is born, to us a son is given, and the government will be on his shoulders. And he will be called Wonderful Counselor, Mighty God, Everlasting Father, Prince of Peace" (Isaiah 9:6).

A child of eight or nine doesn't think of these things. I only knew at the time that I couldn't wait to try out the gift. I remember wolfing down turkey, my mom's special dressing, and pudding so thick you could hear it hit bottom. And I recall tiptoeing after my brother as he headed down the hallway that afternoon. I locked an arrow in place, took careful aim, and pulled on the string until it was tight.

"Hey, Tim!" I yelled. "Merry Christmas!"

And I wondered just for a moment if I should ask permission or forgiveness.

29

Lifestyle of Laughter

It is often just as sacred to laugh as it is to pray.
—CHARLES SWINDOLL

My friend Mike Meaney is a below-the-knee double amputee whose spirit helps him walk faster than most people you'll meet. "My life is not really much different now than it was before," says Mike. "Sure, I have to put on legs in the morning, take them off at night, and have them adjusted periodically. I stumble more than I want. But my wife, Marie, and I travel the world as missionaries, working mainly in Africa—a country lacking in smooth paths and roads."

From the beginning, Mike's challenge has been a haven of humor and good stories. Recently he wrote out for me seven blessings of being a double amputee:

1. I can be as tall as I want.

2. I save lots of money on athlete's-foot spray.

3. I can wear the same socks for weeks at a time.

4. Two years after purchase, my shoes still smell like new leather. Don't try this with yours!

5. If you and I are alone in a room together and we smell dirty feet, we know who to blame!

6. When you're in an airport at the end of a line waiting for customs and you see this guy being whisked directly through the turnstiles very quickly, it might be me!

7. At Christmastime people want me to take them shopping so they can take advantage of my handicapped parking permit.

While in Zambia recently, Mike was being driven through the capital of Lusaka with a gallon and a half of white paint between his feet for a project he was working on. Suddenly his African friend, Pastor Mtonga, veered to the left, quickly upsetting the paint and completely covering both of Mike's shoes. By the time they arrived home, the paint was dry and new shoes were imperative. The next day Mike's friend took him to a market in Lusaka to purchase new ones. Noting that the market was huge and would require much walking, Pastor Mtonga offered to find some shoes and bring them back to the car. But what size? Shoe sizes are different in Africa. Mike immediately took off both of his feet by way of thumbscrews on his ankles, and off went his friend with both of Mike's feet in his arms. Thirty minutes later he returned with newly shoed feet and ten Africans who just had to meet this man who could "send in" his feet for a sale.

A laugh a day, says Mike, keeps the psychiatrist away. Here are an entire month's worth of laughs to pin to your fridge.

Ad in newspaper: Nordic Track $300. Hardly Used. Call Chubbie Hamilton.

Found: dirty white dog. Looks like a rat. Been out awhile. Better be a reward.

Free: farm kittens. Ready to eat.

On IKEA assembly instructions: It is better to be two people during assembly.

Ground beast: 99¢/lb.

For sale: complete set of Encyclopedia Brittanica. $1000 OBO. No longer needed. Got married last weekend. Wife knows everything.

Amana washer $100. Owned by clean bachelor who seldom washed.

Favorite Bumper Snickers:

Honk if you love peace and quiet.

If everything's coming your way, perhaps you're in the wrong lane.

Bills travel through the mail at twice the speed of checks.

The hardness of butter is directly proportional to the softness of the bread.

The sooner you fall behind, the more time you'll have to catch up.

Change is inevitable except from vending machines.

If you think nobody cares, try missing a couple of payments.

The early bird may get the worm, but the second mouse gets the cheese.

As long as there are tests, there will be prayer in public schools.

Where there's a will, I want to be in it!

Warning: dates on calendar are closer than they appear.

> "I stopped believing in Santa Claus when my mother took me to see him in a department store and he asked for my autograph."
>
> —Actress Shirley Temple

Mary Richards: It's a lousy business we're in, Mr. Grant.
I quit. I'm going to Africa to work with Schweitzer.
Lou Grant: Mary, Albert Schweitzer is dead.
Mary Richards: You see what I mean, Mr. Grant? It's a
lousy, lousy world.

—THE *MARY TYLER MOORE SHOW*

Margaret Reutner of Gillette, Wyoming, says her mother
was getting the Thanksgiving turkey ready for the oven. Her
granddaughter Chay walked in, looked at the turkey in the
sink, and announced to everyone, "That looks like you in
the bathtub, Grandma!" Grandmother said without a
moment of hesitation, "You're absolutely right!"

A family in the U.S. Air Force went to the base's
chapel shortly after arriving at their new home.
After the service the chaplain was greeting everyone at the exit, and he said to one of the younger
children, "I understand from your father that you
are Baptists." The child replied, "No, sir, we're
Christians."

—GEORGE COFFEY

Elementary school children at Columbus' Beck School and
Dublin's Chapman Elementary were asked to study a list of
20 axioms with key words missing and fill in the blanks.
Here are a few of my favorites:

If you can't stand the heat, get a *pool.*
A bird in the hand is *messy.*
You can't teach an old dog new *math.*
When in Rome, do *bulls run around town?*
If you can't stand the heat, get *out of the oven.*

A fool and his money are *my best friends.*
A penny saved is *one cent.*
Look before you *run into a pole.*
A rolling stone *makes you flat.*

Bad Day?

I was having a particularly rotten day when I opened the paper and read the following story. A woman came home to find her husband in the kitchen, shaking frantically with what looked like a wire running from his waist towards the electric kettle. Intending to jolt him away from the deadly current, she grabbed a plank of wood from outside the back door and whacked him good. So good that she broke his arm in two places. Imagine his surprise. Until she hit him, he had been happily cleaning the kitchen. And listening to his Walkman. Somehow my day didn't seem so bad, after all.

> *The most wasted of all days is that*
> *during which one has not laughed.*
> —NICOLAS DE CHAMFORT

> *No one need be downcast, for Jesus*
> *is the joy of heaven, and it is His joy*
> *to enter into sorrowful hearts.*
> —FREDERICK WILLIAM FABER
> (1814–1863)

> *The Lord gives His people perpetual joy when they*
> *walk in obedience to Him.*
> —D.L. MOODY (1837–1899)

PART FIVE

It's Better to Live Rich Than to Die Rich

I am wealthy in my friends.

—William Shakespeare

Loneliness is the first thing which God's eye named not good.

—John Milton

30

A Few Good Guys

The next best thing to being wise oneself is to live in a circle of those who are.
—C.S. LEWIS

While researching this book, I asked a few hundred people, "Has your current pace of life affected your relationships positively or negatively?" Only 12 percent answered "positively." Several said they were "losing touch" with others. Many attached notes to the surveys. Here is a small sampling:

"You get high on being so busy you avoid times of intimacy, strolling beside a river, sitting on a park bench, or cuddling in front of the fireplace. Staying on frantic schedules makes life seem to last longer, but the wear and tear eats you alive. One day you wake up with a stranger, the one you used to be married to, or the one you aren't married to at all."

"I now conduct friendships in mini-morsel bites—a few minutes here and there, a passing smile, and a word at church—never enough time to really share and become close to people."

"The increase in pace has caused me to spend less time with family and friends and, of course, with God."

"The speed at which I am living has produced misunderstandings in relationships that had to be solved with the help of a mediator."

"I woke up one day realizing how much I've missed of life. My kids are almost adults. I've reached midlife and haven't yet done anything significant with my hobby."

"I miss the long phone calls in the morning with my sisters."

"I have few relationships outside work and church. Just a friendship with the folks next door seems almost impossible."

"One morning I looked down at our nine-month-old daughter and noticed that she was doing all sorts of new things. I commented to my wife, 'When did she start doing that?' Her answer was a sobering, 'She's been doing that for a while; you probably just didn't notice.'"

"It has affected our marriage. Many times we're actually busy doing things together, but when the busy times cause stress, it definitely makes things chillier around the house."

"Unless people are on e-mail, we probably don't communicate much with them."

"My relationship with God has suffered. *An Gorta Mor* is Gaelic for 'great hunger'—something I've been experiencing lately."

"I know that relationships make my life rich, but I've become too busy to invest in friendship."

One of the greatest dangers of a fast-forward world is that we are programmed to expect things instantly. A radio ad invites us to learn to speed-read a dozen books a day. Thousands of Web sites entice us to get rich quick. Yet the reality is that little of lasting value comes quickly. Instant coffee is a lousy substitute for a long and lingering brew. The best marriages are built on time and trust. Friendships, like houseplants, require nurture and care and constant watering.

A few years ago, I began to realize that many of those I considered my best friends had moved far away, and if things were going to change, I would have to change them. So one morning I asked a new friend out for coffee and popped the question. "Hey," I said, past a mouthful of muffin, "how about we get some guys together a few times a month for a reading group? We'll discuss something serious, like Plato... or Archie. We can meet at my house."

The idea was met with a stifled yawn. "Phil," he said, "I'm busier than a wasp at a barbecue. Besides, a reading club sounds about as exciting as watching cheese mold."

"Well," I stammered, "how about we...uh...how about we get together and just eat. Ya, that's it. An eating club. We'll sample desserts, then have a lively discussion to burn off the calories."

"Now you're talking," said my new friend, squeezing the creamer way too hard. "Sorry about that...here's a napkin."

It's been four years since I cleaned that shirt. Four years since the Circle of Six began convening almost every other Tuesday. For reasons of international security, I can't say much, but I will tell you that each member has agreed to adhere to some strict guidelines as laid out in our red Principles and Procedures notebook:

Rule #1: Be there at 8:30 P.M. Unless you're late.
Rule #2: Hosts will be selected in alphabetic sequence. If you are hosting the event, bake something. We reserve the right to watch you eat it first. If you choke, lose consciousness, or die, we will try to revive you. We will not, however, eat your baking.
Rule #3: If you bring a cell phone, we will take it apart and hide the pieces.

PART OF ME WANTS TO HELP YOU WITH YOUR PROBLEMS, BOB, BUT THE OTHER PART OF ME WANTS TO GO GOLFING.

Rule #4: No talking about Amway or Mannatech. Unless you have a really good story about someone who sells it.
Rule #5: The food must be better than last time we were at your house. If this means your wife bakes it, that's okay. No, your wife may not attend the meeting.
Rule #6: When we run out of food and things to say, the assembly is adjourned.

Tonight we're meeting by candlelight for my wife's cheesecake. It is available in three flavors: Strawberry Slam, Triple Raspberry Rage, and Death by Chocolate. Helpings come in three sizes—the Ballerina, the Allegro, and the Cardiac Arrest. Collectively, we have gained more than 100 pounds in four years of Tuesdays. None of us quite knows why. We've also gained some friends. I wish you could meet these guys. A nicer bunch you're unlikely to find. A better-looking, wealthier bunch, perhaps. But these are the kind of friends you'd crawl through a minefield for. If I were heading into battle, well, I would take some Marines. But I'd want these guys to bring the cheesecake.

When I think of real guys, I think of Vance, Ron, Harold, James, and Glenn. And I think of the following characteristics:

Graceful. You should see these guys swoop down on a dessert. Such speed, grace, and elegance is seldom glimpsed outside ballet halls. But they are also full of grace when it comes to conversation. This is not Gossip 101. This is Sinners Anonymous. Overwhelmed by God's grace, we are looking for ways to pass it on. We do not spend our evenings pointing out the shortcomings of others, because we have encountered a few of our own. We also know that when you point a finger, four fingers are pointing toward you.

Understanding. Though we have come frighteningly close to tears on two occasions, if you come here looking for hugs and sensitivity, you may be disappointed. But if you're looking for some timely advice, or a listening ear, it's great to be surrounded by a few wise guys. In the Psalms, David prays often for understanding. In Psalm 119:34, he asks God, "Give me understanding, and I will keep your law and obey it with all my heart."

Yielded. We sometimes disagree on child rearing or music or automobile brands. But we share one thing in common. Each of us has handed the steering wheel over to God. Yes, we sometimes want to take it back or offer suggestions on how to drive. But we're learning. Together.

Successful. Tonight we got to talking about Stuff we wish we had. About riding mowers, and power sprayers, and hot tubs. Then we laughed. Though it's easy to forget, success is not defined by the stuff we grab, but by the footprints we leave. Our incomes don't define success. Our legacy does.

It was slow going at first. Guys aren't always comfortable talking about what's really happening in our lives. We hide behind the weather and the New York Yankees. But before long someone removes his catcher's mask and admits that he's just an old sinner in need of God's grace. And before you know it the clock strikes midnight and you're all sitting around wishing it hadn't.

Tonight we talk about a friend's failed marriage and what it takes to keep the flame burning. After we say goodnight, I sit on the sofa wishing that every guy on earth had this many friends. Guys who love to laugh. Guys who know that burdens are lighter and the path a whole lot brighter when traveled with a few fat friends.

Now, it's time to clean candle wax off my wife's tablecloth. And, oh yes, I need to do something with this last piece of cheesecake.

31

Connecting Points

Fellow citizens, why do you turn and scrape every
stone to gather wealth, and take so little care of
your children, to whom one day you must
relinquish it all?

—SOCRATES (469–399 B.C.)

"Dad, will you throw the ball with me?" The question lands in the midst of an important newscast, at the end of a grueling day, from a child who stands before me, a weathered glove in one hand, a worn baseball in the other. "Dad, will ya?"

Now, I am not the sharpest knife in the drawer, but I've been watching how quickly my children are growing. We keep a little chart in the pantry that gives us the inch by inch details. The boys are sprouting about an inch every six weeks right now and if they keep it up, they will surpass 18 feet by the time they're my age. A basketball scholarship is not out of the question.

Two or three feet above the chart, I have pasted a cutout of a blackbird. I'm not sure why. I suppose it signifies the arrival of independence. One day these children will soar from this sheltering tree. But for now, as often as I'm able, I won't say no to such requests.

"Dad, will ya?"

You bet I will.

When our children are two, three, and four, we think they will stay this way forever. That diapers and midnight emergencies and acres of luggage will accompany us throughout life. Parents of small children seem to have a special God-given shutoff mechanism when it comes to screaming. They don't hear it the way older people do. Perhaps they are numb from lack of sleep and from sipping Children's Tylenol. But one day the Tylenol wears off and the screaming stops and we wake up and the children are carrying their own luggage.

So wherever we are, we must listen to life, and if we do, we will find daily reminders that we are not here for long. That we were made for more than this.

"Mama, you have cracks in your face!" I heard a small boy say in church once as he stood on his mother's lap. Half the church heard the child too, much to the mother's dismay. Perhaps she is still hiding under the pew. Or perhaps she is longing for the good old days when her child attended church at all.

I must admit that I have held tightly to these child-rearing years. Some parents can't wait to taste the freedom of an empty house. Not me. Oh, it will have its advantages, I'm sure. The walls will be cleaner, our nerves and the carpet less frayed. But for the most part, I've enjoyed these years immensely. And even now I hold the children as close as they'll let me, play catch when they ask, and read out loud books they enjoy. We just finished two biographies, those of Joni Eareckson Tada and Franklin Graham.

Last night I lay awake thinking of the size of our house and how little sense four bedrooms will make ten years from now. I walked into my daughter's bedroom and prayed for her with a lump in my throat. This season of our lives is quickly changing colors. I don't step on little Lego land mines any longer. The dolls are in the hope chest, the stuffed animals rounded up and put away.

Yet, I am aware that at every stage of life, in all of our relationships, we can find connecting points. It may be a ball glove today, a book tomorrow, a soccer ball next week. It may be a hobby, a craft, or a particular topic of discussion. A connecting point is something you both enjoy. My wife and I connect in many areas. Shopping is not one of them. I get a throbbing headache the moment we park the car. I believe there are health hazards in the mall, chemicals released slowly over time, forcing husbands to say such things as, "Yes dear," and "Whatever you say." So my wife and I connect elsewhere.

The new season is bright with possibilities. My children are young adults now. We converse, we disagree, and sometimes I discover that they are right. I suppose in some way they have taught me more than I've taught them. About life. About God. I was taught to dread the teenage years, but I'm enjoying my children more than ever.

This past Thursday, my son Stephen turned 15. We will have three teenagers soon. If you think to pray for us, we just may be needing it. A week before his birthday, I asked Stephen what he wanted if he was lucky enough to have me give him a gift. He didn't pause for a second. "Golf clubs," he said.

I said, "How about something that doesn't cost any money?" But he wouldn't hear of it. So I started looking. I found some Callaway golf clubs. My great-uncle Eli 13 times removed owns the company. But he doesn't return my mail. The clubs start at $2800. Then you need an $800 driver and a $100 putter, and you should probably buy a bag and some tees and some funny-looking pants. Of course, I couldn't afford this, but I did find a rather inexpensive set that I would have given my left arm for as a kid. When Stephen pulled the wrapping off on Thursday, I had to peel him from the ceiling.

You see, the golf course is a connecting point for the two of us. It's something we both enjoy. Connecting points. Find them in all of your relationships. It may be a baseball mitt, a hobby, or hitting balls on a golf course. Twice a week or so Stephen and I find ourselves talking about things we didn't intend to when we walk side by side down to the creek to look for my ball. We talk about girls, about movies, about girls, and best of all, sometimes we find ourselves talking about Jesus. And I tell Stephen that I don't care if he makes a ton of money or becomes prime minister of Canada or the CEO of AOL.com, but if he walks with Jesus, I'll be the most thankful guy alive.

32

You've Got E-Mail

I miss the tangible world of letters,
slitting open the envelopes, unfolding the pages.
I miss their individuality, the personality
that rides the curve of the ink.
—Susan Lendroth in Newsweek

Most of us can remember the first time someone tapped us on the shoulder and said, "Hey, there's a letter for you." For me the event took place in first grade, when the government mistakenly drafted me for the Vietnam War. But still I was happy to get a letter from someone. I loved the mailbox. Still do. I don't mean the *Reader's Digest* sweepstakes offer or the fund-raising letter from the Society for the Protection of Societies, but an actual letter written just to you. For many of us, it's been a long time, hasn't it? The mailbox may bulge with coupon packs, bills, and limited-time offers, but personal letters are as rare as an evening at the opera with Willie Nelson.

I suppose we are witnessing the end of an era, and if I sound too nostalgic, I hope you will indulge me for a few moments. I suppose the nostalgia comes from the fact that my wife and I dated through the mailbox. Although we lived

HOW CAN YOU SAY WE DON'T COMMUNICATE?
I SENT YOU AN E-MAIL JUST YESTERDAY!

in the same town, we wrote weekly letters, most of which Ramona has kept to this day. We read through some the other night amid generous laughter and even a few tears. The letters chronicled a thousand things we had forgotten and reminded us of a few things we were glad to forget.

In those days I checked my mailbox eagerly. You never knew. One day I received an envelope that said, "Snake Eggs: Use Caution." When I slit the envelope, something jumped out at me. It was a simple contraption, a paper clip wound with a rubber band, but I didn't stop shaking for hours. I married the girl who sent it to me, and there have been a few more surprises along the way. Most of them good ones.

At the age of ten I fell in love with a postage stamp collector's book and became pen pals with people in exotic countries such as Zimbabwe, Czechoslovakia, and Arkansas. I suppose the stamp book would be worth a fortune today, wherever it is. Through the years, letters have linked me to friends who moved away and family members who travel, but most of the letters have stopped coming. We get in touch in other ways, or not at all.

Somewhere the world changed. The long-distance rates plummeted, e-mail took off, and the letters stopped. Christmas letters and missionary updates still come. But they are mass-produced now, which saves time, I suppose. I am as guilty as the next guy. E-mail is quick, it is business-friendly, and it becomes history with the press of a button.

But something is missing. How I loved the personal touch of a letter. The paper laced with perfume. A card concealing a stick of gum. A tangible reminder that someone thought of me enough to spend a whopping eight cents on a postage stamp.

When I was a boy, my father was in the public relations business. Part of his job was to handle angry letters addressed to the ministry where he worked. One night I overheard him talking to Mom about a letter he had received that day. "Remember the Three-Day Rule," Mother said. Dad nodded. I was curious about the rule, so I asked. "When you write anything negative in a letter," Mom told me, "it's a good idea to let it sit in a drawer for three days. Then read it again and decide whether you should fix it. That's our rule."

Though I use e-mail regularly, I've tried to remember that rule. Twice I have sent things I wish I hadn't: once it took a long trip to fix it, the other time a phone call. By its nature, e-mail seems to fight our need to stop and contemplate what we are saying, to carefully consider our words. As a Christian, I am to be a person of the spoken and written word. My words should build up, encourage, and strengthen others. This doesn't always come quickly. It requires time.

A pastor friend told me that his church was split apart when e-mails—many containing gossip, slander, and sharply worded personal attacks against him—were forwarded literally around the world. He had two alternatives. The first was to place the following on his answering machine: "Hello, you have reached the church office. If you wish to criticize last Sunday's sermon, press one. To complain about the music, press two. To blast the youth pastor, press three. If you have a word of encouragement, the pastor will be right with you." Instead, he included in the bulletin some helpful rules for electronic communication:

1. Never write anything you would not want the entire world to read.

2. Never use e-mail to confront, correct, or confess. Always do this in person. Never reply to such e-mail. Ask for a personal meeting instead.

3. Use e-mail to exchange factual information only.

4. If you want to send your love, encouragement, or support, meet in person or write a letter.

5. Let all your speech be seasoned by love and full of grace.

Recently I made an effort to turn back the tide of e-mails by writing letters to three friends. I didn't use perfume, but I made sure the letters were handwritten. Within a week each of the three friends had answered. All of them by e-mail.

A few months ago, missionary friends of ours in the Philippines e-mailed to tell me that their son was seriously ill. He loved my books, said the mother, and she asked if I'd be able to send her son, Kyle, something from Canada. Flattery will get you everywhere, so I sent him a package: "Snake Eggs: Use Caution." Not really. Instead, our family put together a small packet of Canadian goods for him.

Six weeks later, amid the usual bills and fund-raising appeals, I discovered to my delight a brown parcel festooned with bright blue Filipino stamps and secured by a thin red ribbon. Eagerly I snipped the parcel open at one end. Five packages fell out on my desk. Dried mangoes and pineapples labeled "To Die For." Flavored nuts ranging from "Mild" to "Mother-In-Law Hot Pepper."

Within minutes I sent the following e-mail:

Dear Forest and Carol,

You won't believe what arrived in my mailbox today. Wow! It is moments like these when being a Christian is tough. I would like to lock myself in a room somewhere and savor them all by myself, but I would miss the joy of bringing them out of my briefcase at supper tonight and watching the expressions on the children's faces and seeing my wife go straight for those mangoes while I tell her that she'll have to kiss me on the lips first.

Thanks so much. You are wonderful. I was thrilled to hear that Kyle is doing better. Smack him between the shoulder blades for me! May the Lord continue to strengthen all of you as you serve Him there.

100,000 Blessings!

Phil

Would you do something for me before you read the next chapter? Would you take five minutes to scribble a note to someone you haven't written to in more than a year?

Then drop it in an envelope and mail it tomorrow.

Just don't try to mail it with an eight-cent stamp.

33

Ten Things I Used to Hate About You

Son: Is it true, Dad? I heard that in some parts of Africa a man doesn't know his wife until he marries her.

Dad: That happens in this country too, son.

The healthiest relationships are those that breathe—that move out and then move back together.
—JAMES DOBSON

Six months before my wedding day, an older man tapped my shoulder in the post office and offered some free advice. "Ramona's a lovely girl," he said, licking a stamp. "She deserves a good husband. Marry her before she finds one."

And that's what I decided to do. But before Ramona agreed, she sat me down one Sunday after church, placed my hands on a Bible and asked me the usual questions:

a. You are pretty good at basketball, Phil, but have you ever in your life been able to hit a laundry hamper?

b. Will you refrain from using phrases like "I told you so," "I never had to *chew* my mother's tomato soup," or "Is there anything to eat around here"?

c. Will you agree to take me shopping once a year just for fun? Will you pace the floors while I am in the fitting room, or will you relax a little?

I didn't feel comfortable lying to her right there in the sanctuary, so we retreated to the parking lot where I kissed her deeply and agreed to work on these things.

Six months later we stood at an altar as a preacher peppered me with more questions: "Wilt thou take this woman to be thy lawful wedded wife, Phil? Will you rinse the sink when you shave and make the bed when you're the last one out of it? Will you forget baseball statistics and remember her birthday? Will you affirm, admire, and accept her—and quit eating chicken wings with a fork, so long as you both shall live?"

I kissed her deeply. And agreed to work on these things.

Minutes later, as I stood in the receiving line watching people I'd never met kiss my bride, the same man who approached me in the post office whispered some more advice. "She looks mighty fine today," he said, "but she will drive you nuts sometimes. I've been married 56 years. I should know." Leaning closer, he tapped my shoulder with his cane. "You want a happy marriage?" he said. "When the things that attracted you to her start to drive you apart, find a way to reverse the process."

I've been thinking about the old man's advice for 18 years now, and it's finally starting to make sense. Allow me to explain.

When Ramona and I were dating, I was attracted to her many attributes, including the way she took life slowly. I was constantly running. She taught me to stop and taste the strawberries. Three weeks after our honeymoon, the lack of speed with which she approached life made my adrenaline race. I found myself sitting in the car Sunday mornings tapping the dashboard, resisting the urge to honk. By the time we got to church, worship was the furthest thing from either of our minds. But 18 years have brought me full circle. In a world that's on permanent fast-forward, my wife is a living illustration that slowing down is not only enviable, it is possible. And perhaps it's even possible, as the old man discovered, for the things that drive us nuts to drive us together.

That doesn't mean I've come to peace with everything she does. Early on I wanted to follow Martin Luther's example and nail a List of Irritations to the bathroom door. I couldn't quite come up with 95 theses, but ten came to mind:

1. Your sense of humor is warped. The funniest thing I did this week was hit my head on a cupboard door. You laughed as if I were Peter Sellers. This was not funny to me at the time. It still isn't. Please do not laugh when you read this.

2. A vow of silence is fine for a monk. Our late-night "fights" are as one-sided as a Chicago Cubs game. You grow quiet during arguments. Silence can be a virtue, but it can also be maddening.

3. You are kind to phone salesmen. On our first anniversary a phone call interrupted a candlelight dinner I had prepared. You walked away from a perfectly good (albeit rather burned) pizza to talk for upwards of two minutes to a complete stranger because you were too polite to hang up.

4. Generosity isn't always a virtue. Last week you made four pies and gave away three. Our tithe to the church now exceeds the 10 percent solution Jacob recommended in Genesis 28. You gave ten dollars to the Girl Scouts and the cookies weren't that great.

5. What's next, pickle ice cream? On Wednesday you made banana meat loaf. Meat loaf is bad enough without the fruit. What other recipes do you have? Can we go through them together?

6. Morning is broken. I am a night owl, you rise with the sun. You delight in greeting me early and releasing the blind loudly. Unfortunately, I do not wake up until noon. Please do not sing to me before 8 A.M.—even on my birthday.

7. You are a cheapskate. I wanted to buy a new car and you said, "Sure, or shall we just light 3000 dollar bills on fire?" You believe we shouldn't spend more than we make. If this were true, why did they invent credit cards?

8. You throw things away. Last week my wool sweater went missing. The one I got for my seventh birthday. If I don't glue things down, they walk away. When we have children will you package them up and send them to the Salvation Army?

9. Necking won't fit on the calendar. I love to do things we haven't planned. Like quick trips to the city, surprise purchases, or necking on a back road to nowhere. You like the necking, but you like to plan for it.

10. I am from Switzerland, you are from Zimbabwe. I love to be on time. You do not. Is this a cultural difference? Meet me in the living room at 8 P.M. sharp and we'll talk about it.

After some thought, I did not nail the list to our bathroom door, and it is a good thing. Through the years we have had numerous discussions on each point, and 18 years in the University of Diversity have taught me that if we were the same we'd be in trouble. If we were both spenders, we'd be bankrupt. If we were both spontaneous, we'd never get anything done. If we kept all my wool sweaters, we'd have to rent 13 U-Hauls each time we move.

The Bible describes marriage as two becoming one. Ideally, it is a partnership of two distinctly different individuals who are stronger together than apart. But this won't happen until we swallow our pride, praise each other's uniqueness, and encourage each other's strengths. And a little humor helps too.

Martha Bolton agrees. Like Ramona, her husband, Russ, likes to throws things away. "It wouldn't be so bad," Martha told me, "if he would stop with *his* things. But he throws my things away too. I've had to dig through the trash to find that bank deposit slip on which I had written my next book idea. I've tried paying him back and letting him 'discover' a few of his things (favorite books, day planner, chess set) in the trash too, but he just laughs and doesn't get the connection. This has been a habit with him for so long, I don't know if he'll ever completely give up his compulsion."

Martha's secret? "Just keep loving him…and checking the trash." Better still, she has come to see the benefits of his clutter-free personality. "He doesn't like clutter in our relationship either," says Martha. "He doesn't hold grudges or bring up past issues. If something keeps getting in our way, he'd rather toss it out than continue to hang on to it. It's turned into one of the things I love about him. Of course, I still check the trash every week before the rubbish man takes it away. I've still got deadlines to meet."

Joanne Robideau, a 36-year-old mother and high school teacher, says, "I used to hate the way my husband, Gord, went into things without planning ahead and just did things off the cuff. Now I've learned to appreciate his spontaneous approach to life and how quickly he adapts to situations. I used to get anxious when we would walk into something we hadn't planned for; now I rely on his ability to take over. What I thought was a curse has turned into a blessing."

I agree. Though Ramona's silence caused me grief at first, I'm learning to wait until she's ready to talk and to remind myself that those who say the most do not always have the most to say. When book sales brought in unexpected abundance, it was her generosity that helped us respond as Christ would, giving away what we didn't need. Her kindness to phone salesmen was the same kindness that first drew me to her. Thankfully, it has tempered with time. She now offers a polite "No thanks," followed by a click.

Perhaps best of all, it is her warped sense of humor that allowed me just last week to hang a small blackboard beside the phone. Now each time a telemarketer calls, she says, "Why don't you talk to my husband?" and she holds the phone by the blackboard, grinning while she runs her fingernails over it.

34

The Marriage Quiz

*Getting married is easy. Staying married
is more difficult. Staying happily married
for a lifetime should rank
among the fine arts.*

—Singer Roberta Flack

The following quiz is intended solely for the amusement of our readers. Scores should not be brought up during petty arguments, loud disagreements, or in front of the children. Please answer the questions honestly, bearing in mind that while it is impossible to fail this test, your answers may determine whether or not you spend the night on the couch.

1. When you are wrong, you will admit it to your partner:

   a. Within seconds.

   b. Just as soon as cows produce Coca-Cola.

   c. Usually before sunset.

2. Which of the following most accurately describes the frequency of your lovemaking?

   a. Tri-weekly

   b. Try weakly

   c. Try weekly

3. Complete this sentence: I believe the children of Israel wandered in the wilderness for 40 years because:

   a. God was testing their marriages.

   b. Moses refused to ask his wife for directions.

   c. Moses wanted them to really appreciate the Promised Land once they got there.

4. When you're watching TV together, who controls the remote?

   a. We do not watch television; we go for walks and talk about our feelings.

   b. I do.

   c. Whoever gets it first.

5. The food that best sums up your spouse's kiss:

   a. Red hot chili peppers

   b. Airline omelet

   c. Ice cream and apple pie

6. The movie title that best sums up your sex life:

   a. *Some Like It Hot*

   b. *Gone with the Wind*

   c. *As Good As It Gets*

7. (For men only) You are on your knees giving thanks for the new purchase: a late model minivan, complete with CD player. The phone rings. It is your frenzied wife calling from Biff's Auto Repair to tell you that she has totalled the van. You:

   a. Ask if she's okay.

   b. Total the telephone.

   c. Ask if she's okay...and if the CD player still works.

8. (For women only) After a particularly tough day, your husband has crashed in front of the TV set. You decide to:

   a. Stand beside the TV set and try on lingerie.

   b. Steal his Visa card and go shopping.

   c. Pour two tall ginger ales and crash with him.

9. Your definition of communication is:

   a. I am attentive to my partner's communication needs. I listen well and share openly my thoughts, aspirations, and feelings.

   b. Nintendo.

   c. Sorry, I was distracted. Could you repeat the question?

10. Your 14-year-old daughter asks if she can go on a date. You will:

    a. Explain to her that open communication, trust, dependability, and good character are the determining factors in such a decision; that when she shows all of these characteristics simultaneously and is mature enough to set an example for her little sister she will be permitted to take part in group dating, followed by double dating, both of which will prepare her for the responsibility of single couple dating at a later time, always chaperoned.

    b. Laugh uncontrollably.

    c. Briefly consider installing land mines in the front yard.

11. (For men only) Sunday morning has arrived, but your wife has not. She is still moving about the house checking on appliances—despite the fact that you are once again

late for church. While waiting in the car with the children, you decide to:

   a. Return to the house and ask, "Is there anything I can do to help you, dear? I know I traumatized you this morning by bringing breakfast in bed a little late. I certainly do apologize."

   b. Leave without her.

   c. Help the kids with their memory verses and somehow resist the urge to honk.

12. Aliens from the planet Plutonium have landed on your roof to observe your marriage and file a report. They describe you as:

   a. Inseparable.

   b. Single.

   c. Tired, but fun. So fun I think we should invade their bodies!

13. It's 12:30 A.M. and neither of you can sleep. Your spouse says, "Honey, I'm hungry. Would you get me a slice of cheese?" You say:

   a. "Is that all, sweetheart? How about a salad with croutons?"

   b. "Zzzzzzzzzzzzz."

   c. "How thick shall I slice it?"

How to score: First of all, you have to romance your wife, then...whoops...wrong kind of scoring. If you answered "a" more than six times, thanks for taking this quiz during your honeymoon. We wish you all the best in the years ahead. If you found yourself gravitating to the "b" responses, please take an aspirin and read the next chapter in the morning. Also...find a soft pillow. It's time to sleep on the couch. If you chose "c" five or more times, you've got a good thing going. Collect 17 bonus points if you also answered "a" more than once. Sounds like some flexibility, lots of laughter, and a servant heart are keeping your marriage fresh. Now, break out the ginger ale, it's time to try weekly!

35

Investing in Memories

*Taking the gospel to people wherever they are
is...frontline love. It is our one hope for...restoring
the sense of community, of caring for one another,
that our decadent, impersonalized culture has
sucked out of us.*
—Charles Colson

In February, thanks in part to our great-uncle Air Miles, our family of five spent a week in Mexico, suffering in the sand and pounding the streets of Mazatlan looking for cheap T-shirts. We sampled the local cuisine and interacted with street people—many of them without limbs, most of them without hope. We counted our pennies before going and decided we could wait a year to update our car. "I have yet to regret a dollar I spent making memories," I told my wife. She agreed. I suppose you need money to make a living, but you need memories to make a life.

A week out of school has never been a tough sell to our children (nor to their teachers for some strange reason). One principal told me, "Take them. We haven't had peace around here for years." I'm quite sure he was kidding. "You go," he said, getting a little more serious. "Your kids will learn more in a week there than a month here."

He was right.

On the final night of our vacation we spent 25 pesos on an open-air taxi, complete with a driver who suffered from hoof-and-mouth disease—he drove fast and loved yelling. He also had a craving for loud American music, playing it at 100 decibels through huge speakers lodged between my knees. Shania Twain was feeling like a woman as the taxi bounced along the crumbling concrete. Our children, aged 11 through 14, were grinning from the backseat as I turned to them and crossed my eyes. Next up was the Bloodhound Gang, whose irresponsible lyrics sum up well a culture in decline. The driver turned up the volume, which seemed to have a direct link to my blood pressure. Together we listened to a song that informed my children they are nothing but mammals, so why not do it like they do it on the Discovery Channel. It was a far cry from "I wanna hold your hand." The children's eyes were big as golf balls. Later that night we enjoyed an hour-long balcony discussion about the choices and consequences of such a culture.

The next morning, United Airlines—like a bad saltshaker—sprinkled our family throughout a packed L-1011. My wife is across the aisle. Our daughter in front of her. The boys behind us. Beside me sits Mike, a 19-year-old, and his pretty girlfriend. Mike turns to me. "Did you get drunk a lot down there?" he asks. Most people do not introduce themselves to me this way.

"No," I laugh. "I have too much fun sober. How about you?"

"Man, I love their tequila. I got drunk every night," he says. "It was cool."

"How did you feel in the morning?"

"Oh...I threw up a lot," he winces. "It was awful."

"Not so cool, huh?"

Mike informs me that his girlfriend and he are living together. That they don't want to marry. Both their parents are divorced. I inform him that my wife and I are celebrating our eighteenth year. That there's nothing like sticking together through the tough times. And I grin across the aisle at the only girl I've ever really kissed.

Overhead a movie flickers on the television screen. A movie I would not have chosen. Beside me the topic turns to religion.

"I'm sort of a Buddhist, but sort of, like, a Christian, you know," says Mike. "I kind of like Hinduism too. Most of the big religions are sort of cool. They all have trinities, our professor says." His girlfriend nods and twirls her neck-lace—a cross. "Whatever works," she says.

Mike turns to me. "So what religion are you?"

We are flying over Salt Lake City now. I smile. "I'm not into religion," I say. "I used to be. See out that window? That's the capital city of Mormonism. It's like the others. You follow a long list of rules, you'll be okay. You mess up, you're in trouble. What about you?"

"Well," he says, squinting out the window. "I...um...I'm a combination. We're studying religion at the University. My prof says there's good in everything and we need to be tol-erant, but most of all I guess I'm really getting in touch with myself lately. I guess I just believe in myself."

"Did you ever let yourself down?" I ask with a grin.

"Ya," he smiles reluctantly, "but I'm getting better. I only disappoint myself about 20 percent of the time now." I laugh, but he is serious. "I just think that whatever path you choose, that's cool. You just need to respect yourself. So," he asks, "are you an atheist?"

"No," I laugh, noticing that my daughter is peering back at me with those golf-ball eyes. "There's too much evidence to the contrary."

I am strangely comfortable sitting there. You see, one of the greatest stresses in my life has always come from some-thing Christians call "witnessing." I would sit on an airplane knowing that if it crashed and the guy beside me went to hell, it would be my fault alone. When I told others about my faith, I was as clumsy as a carpenter with ten thumbs. I took a personal evangelism course once to try to get over it, then I tried preaching on the street. A little girl threw rocks at me. I decided to throw *Four Spiritual Laws* booklets from a moving car, but I couldn't bring myself to do it. I knew the authorities might throw me in jail for littering, and I'd have to witness there. In those days, I operated out of guilt, not love. Finally, I realized that a closed mouth gathers no foot, so I kept mine shut.

A few years ago I made a surprising discovery: When I simply tell others what I have seen or what God has done, they listen. When I incorporate some humor, their faces light up and sometimes their hearts do too. I used to count conversions, now I count conversations. I don't have all the right answers, but I know and care about the questions.

"So what are you?" asks Mike, jarring me from my thoughts. "One of those...what do you call 'em...?"

"Agnostics?"

"Ya."

"No...I just have a relationship with Jesus. He's changed everything."

"Oh," he says, "Jesus is cool. He was a good teacher. So was Mohammed."

"Well, I used to think that too. But Jesus can't just be a good teacher."

"What do you mean?"

"Well, is your religion professor a good teacher?"

"He's okay."

"But if he came to class one day and said, 'I have an announcement to make: I'm the Son of God. I'm the way, the truth, and the life: no one comes to God except through me,' what would you think?"

"I'd think he was crazy." Mike pauses, considers for a moment, then sees a light come on: "Oh," he says softly, "I see what you mean."

"Jesus claimed to be the Son of God, Mike. Either He was lying, or He was crazy, or He was right. You have to choose. They didn't crucify Him because He was a nice guy or a good teacher. Either He was a liar, a lunatic, or He's Lord."

Across the aisle my wife's head is bowed. I find out later that Rachael is praying too.

"I think I know the answer." Mike is nodding his head. "He must be Lord."

Down through the centuries, millions of others have come to that same conclusion. That Jesus Christ, God's Son, lived a sinless life, was crucified in our place, and was miraculously raised from the dead. That He defeated death so that we might live with Him forever—and live abundant lives while we are here.

That day, before exiting the plane, we exchanged addresses so I could send Mike and his girlfriend a Bible. And I told them that if my wife starts praying for them, they won't have a chance. They laughed and said they wouldn't mind at all if she did.

When Jesus walked the earth He seemed too busy to be bothered with trivial pursuits and minor issues and the quest for stuff. But He did have time for the two things that really matter. The two things that last forever: God's Word and people.

36

My Best Round Ever

The only time my prayers are never answered
is on the golf course.
—BILLY GRAHAM

For a mere $270, you can golf all year round on the course near our small town. Not that you'd want to. In December here it's colder than a polar bear's kiss, and by January the only people on the course are ice fishermen who sit around fires shivering and dreaming of August. But for three months of summer there's nothing finer than an early morning walk down our narrow fairways, avoiding creeks teeming with catfish and tame deer who have been known to stroll over and check your scorecard.

I've golfed the finest courses in America, from Oregon's coast to Georgia's humidity, but none quite measure up to this nine-hole marvel near home.

Here I learned to golf.

And I've learned a few things about life too.

When I was a boy my father told me to treat my friends as I would my golf clubs. "Take them out often, son," he said, "and never let them beat you." I wasn't sure what he meant at the time (I was only three), but in the past few years

I've come to discover that golf is a team sport. It's best enjoyed with a few good friends.

Of course, not all my friends love to golf. Dan Johnson, for instance, once told me that golf is cow-pasture pool and a poor excuse for a sport. "Football—now there's a sport," said Dan, thumping his chest. "The only way you can get hurt playing golf is to get struck by lightning."

I took Dan golfing one stormy day, and on the par three sixth hole, after he had lost every single white ball in my bag, he was struck, not by lightning, but by the fact that he was wrong. Sometimes golf can hurt you. When we reached the green—a wonderfully nasty green that slopes like a ski hill and that can only be reached by traversing two magnetic creeks—Dan just kept on walking down the cart path, past the clubhouse, and out to the parking lot, where he kicked small stones around with his expensive golf shoes until I arrived.

"Golf is a four-letter word," he said through his teeth.

"I think I'll play six holes every time I come," I told him as we drove home in relative silence. "I shot a 25 today—my best score yet." Dan wasn't finding humor in much of anything. "Golf's no sport," he insisted. "It's an expensive way of playing marbles."

I am thankful not all my friends feel this way. Gord Robideau is an avid golfer in the sense that if he had to choose between playing a round and ensuring world peace, he would want to know how many holes. Gord is a schoolteacher. For him golf is science, art, and physics all rolled into one class. When we play together, the competition is keen. On the first hole, Gord stretches at length before teeing off. Then he tosses tufts of grass in the air, holds a wet finger to the wind, and talks to the ball. "Alright, little buddy," he says, "let's you and me be friends all day. I'll swing...you say 'wonderful.'"

"You know," I tell Gord as we saunter toward the first sand trap, "in the time it takes you to hit the ball I could memorize *War and Peace* in Latin." He laughs. But by the time the eighteenth hole has devoured our Top-Flites and we've compared scores, someone else does all the laughing. I am the winner by two strokes.

Gord and I have an agreement: If he beats me, I buy him lunch. If I beat him, he accuses me of cheating. "You have a special hole in your pocket," he says, as we sip Cokes. "You lost a ball in the rough on number seven, so you released a replacement down your pant leg. I saw you."

"It's okay, Gord," I tell him. "I know how it feels. I once lost in checkers. To a four-year-old."

"You know," he said, putting the tees back in his bag, "you always manage to beat me somehow. But you've never beaten this course."

"What do you mean?"

"You've never parred it."

"Can't be done," I say. "Too much water...fairways slope to the creek...it's uphill even when it's downhill."

"Tell you what," says Gord, with a wide grin. "You par this course and I'll buy you lunch for life...I'll pay your membership next year and throw in some mutual funds."

"Serious?"

"Well, I'm serious about lunch."

Now, please understand that I am a bogey golfer. I am also a cheapskate. So all that winter I practiced in our basement thinking about free lunch. I strung up a net, carpeted a putting green and memorized Arnold Palmer videos. But by June my swing was a mess. By July the course had me beat. And by August I'd salted away my clubs.

Then came the phone call. It was Dan Johnson. "Let's go golfing," he said.

"You okay, Dan?" I answered. "Did they switch your medication?"

"Naw, I'd...well...I'd just like to get away for a few hours. I need someone to talk to."

Dan drove the cart that day. And told me of his marriage. Of his life. The mistakes behind him. The changes ahead. Sometimes he pulled out a club, but mostly he talked. I golfed. And listened. On the sixth hole we sat on the grass of the tee-off box, talking about golf and about life. "The thing I love about golf," I told him, "is that each day is a fresh start. That's how it is with grace too. In our lives. In our marriages. We won't get perfect scores, but grace gives us another chance. Grace gives us hope."

Standing up, I pulled a six-iron from my bag and hit the straightest shot of my life, 162 yards over two greedy creeks. It landed two feet from the pin, spun backward, clung momentarily to the lip of the cup, and came to rest an inch from the hole. Dan watched in amazement.

"What's your score so far?" he asked.

"I haven't a clue," I said. "I don't dare think about it."

All day I didn't miss a shot. I sank three 15-foot putts, my pitching wedge made beautiful music, my driver was a laser beam. As we sipped pop, Dan tallied my score and gasped in amazement: I was two under. Grabbing a cell phone, I called Gord.

"Ha, not a chance," he said.

"I have a witness," I said. "Dinner tonight?"

"Okay. Dinner tonight."

It's been two years since that roast beef dinner and the round of my life. I haven't come close to par since. But I've been thinking about it. And wondering if the best things happen when we are thinking of others. Celebrating friendship. And talking about grace.

37

The Best Investment

*You can choose to be a bag of
marbles...independent, hard, loud,
unmarked, and unaffected by others. Or
you can be a bag of grapes...fragrant, soft,
blending, mingling, flowing into one another's lives.
Marbles are made to be counted and kept.
Grapes are made to be bruised and used.*
—CHARLES SWINDOLL

It was one of the worst days of my life—the
washing machine broke down, the telephone kept
ringing, my head ached, and the mail carrier
brought a bill I had no money to pay. Almost to
the breaking point, I lifted my one-year-old into
his high chair, leaned my head against the tray,
and began to cry. Without a word, my son
took his pacifier out of his mouth and stuck it in
mine.
—RUTH OSHINS

Somehow I had this idea that when our kids grew
up and left home, we would have more relaxation
time. What a joke! Our son is in his second year
at Bible college and our daughter in her first. We
seem to be very busy with just two of us. But we

are also doing things we enjoy. Like increasing our visiting. Now that we are not needed at home, we feel freer to drop in on friends or go out for coffee. With two TVs in the house and no kids to share with, we each have a TV to watch, but we choose not to do that. We watch something together—even during the playoffs.

—CAROLYN GRAHAM

In Africa, relationship comes before time. Before getting any information from a person, you need to find out how they are. Believe me, you expect more than "Fine, thank you." You discover how their family is doing and far more than you may want to know. When we moved from South Africa (which is pretty first world in its demands) to the little kingdom of Lesotho, we were constantly frustrated with how long meetings and appointments took. So you can imagine how fast things seemed to us when we moved to America three years ago. We have had to learn to say no, or let me think about it…to realize that our children will develop normally without all the extra activities, that there is a need for my husband and me to be alone together. Our cell group members observed a natural progression: "Come on over anytime. Let's have a meal together." "Come grab a quick cup of coffee." "We'll meet you at Starbucks." "I'll give you a call sometime." "I'll e-mail you." As a couple we have made it our practice to always allow our door to be open. Sometimes this is hard, but there is always a blessing in being there for others.

—TRACY THOMPSON

I've had to become much more intentional about devoting time to connecting with those closest to me, since we no longer have as many spontaneous times to spend together. Also, I've concentrated more on keeping up with fewer people. I'm trying to do a better job of keeping up with others, but doing so with fewer people.

—RON LEE

Wrap the TV in bubble pack as though you are moving to some romantic isle, and let it sit there. Next, let your dog bury the remote without your following him or spying on the location. Learn to read again while eating that before-bed tummy soother—the bowl of cereal—quietly at a table. There is an additional benefit. If you are married and you give up TV to honor your spouse, you will not only slow your pace instantly, but you will also notice the world around you in a more lively way. People actually talk, smile, and say things worth listening to. They are huggable and full of things to laugh over. Colors are much truer. You become more aware of life in slow motion to such an extent that you feel much younger without having to work at it. The icing on the cake, so to speak, is that your wife will cease being too busy for you, and you can rediscover the one you used to know.

—PAUL STEINHAUER

We have made a decision as a couple to limit our commitments. We are out as a couple only one school night a week. We find if one of us isn't home, the kids don't do their chores or their homework, and they eat all the food in the house! Also, from a relationship side, our kids are very important to us, and we want to be spending time with them.

—CYNDI CHOMICK

When you have Christ, you are rich.
He is enough...People change and fail...
But Christ is eternally faithful.

—THOMAS À KEMPIS

(C. 1380–1471)

PART SIX

Live So the Preacher Won't Have to Lie at Your Funeral

How shall we rest in God? By giving ourselves wholly to Him. If you give yourself by halves, you cannot find full rest; there will ever be a lurking disquiet in that half that is withheld. Martyrs, confessors, and saints have tasted this rest, and "counted themselves happy in that they endured." A countless host of God's faithful servants have drunk deeply of it under the daily burden of a weary life—dull, commonplace, painful, or desolate. All that God has been to them He is ready to be to you. The heart once fairly given to God, with a clear conscience, a fitting rule of life, and a steadfast purpose of obedience, you will find a wonderful sense of rest coming over you.

—Jean-Nicolas Grou (1731–1803)

38

Getting Real

A commentary of the times is that the word
honesty *is now preceded by* old-fashioned.
—LARRY WOLTERS

According to pollster George Barna, the greatest stress in life comes from living what you do not believe. It is a statement worth considering.

During a graveside service, a widow and her son stood near the casket as the minister applauded the life of their husband and father. The truth was, the husband had neglected the two of them to pursue wealth, and they hardly knew him. But the minister had been informed otherwise. Standing with black notebook in one hand, he read a glowing and lengthy tribute to the deceased, noting his contributions to society, the business world, his country, and home. Finally, after listening to about 15 minutes of these accolades, the widow bent over to her son and said, "Go see who's in the casket. I think they've got the wrong man."

Every one of us, if we're honest, will admit that there are times when we feel like the wrong man, or the wrong woman.

One of the mixed blessings of public speaking is listening to the way people introduce you. It's sometimes best to cover your ears. You wonder who they're talking about. Of course the one doing the introducing is merely relaying what he or she has read or heard, but sometimes I wonder what it would sound like if someone who knew me well did the introducing. My friend Vance would probably introduce me this way:

> Phil is a pretty normal guy. He has an awful slice when he golfs, and his wife practices what he preaches. He has, on occasion, yelled at his kids, and he once yelled at me for starting a rototiller outside his window on a Sunday afternoon. I know for a fact that he loves his wife, but he also frustrates her at times, to the point where Ramona has twice considered scrambling an egg on his head. He loves Jesus, but sometimes he gives way to covetousness, jealousy, hypocrisy, and self-righteousness. I have seen him at his worst, but I've also seen him ask for forgiveness. Phil is a sinner saved by grace. God loves him. I sometimes do. And I hope today that you will too.

I think I'd like that. The truth is, I have lived much of my life a hypocrite, and it's hard work. In the church where I grew up (I actually grew up at home, but you know what I mean), hypocrisy was rewarded well. I learned early that looking right and talking right was all I needed to do to get by. But if I stepped out of line or started asking tough questions, it was like water-skiing uphill with a 200-pound backpack. I thank God for parents who were real, who taught me that God looks past the outward appearance. But I must admit that hypocrisy dies hard. Today I consider myself a recovering Pharisee, constantly aware of my tendency to judge others, daily aware of my need for God's grace.

There is abundant peace and rest in being real. Pretending is hard work. While waiting for a flight recently, I watched a man hide behind a newspaper as a woman passed him. He kept glancing her direction, wondering if she'd return, terror written on his face. There is no greater stress than that of running from our past or living a lie.

In 1 Timothy 1:16, the apostle Paul refers to himself as "the worst of sinners," the chief of sinners, the head honcho. In Romans 7:19, he admits, "For what I do is not the good I want to do; no, the evil I do not want to do—this I keep on doing." Such an admission brings us to our knees, and surprisingly, brings freedom, joy, and peace.

After the disgraced televangelist Jimmy Bakker released his book *I Was Wrong,* I spent a few hours with him talking about his time in prison. I couldn't help but think that the worst prison he had ever been in was the self-imposed prison of hypocrisy and self-righteousness.

When John Lennon was shot outside the Dakota building in New York City back in 1980, the former Beatle left behind him $550 million. But what did he really leave behind? In *Time* magazine, his son Julian said, "The only thing my dad taught me was how not to be a father." Later, in a lengthy interview in the *Calgary Herald,* he elaborated. "From my point of view, I felt he was a hypocrite," said Julian, the son of Lennon and his first wife Cynthia, who was abandoned by his father when Julian was five. "Dad could talk about peace and love out loud to the world, but he could never show it to the people who supposedly meant the most to him—his wife and son. How can you talk about peace and love and have a family in bits and pieces—no communication, adultery, divorce? You can't do it, not if you're being true and honest with yourself."

Those words should cause all of us to stop and ponder our footprints. What are we really leaving behind?

I don't watch David Letterman often, but one night he was interviewing political analyst, author, and talk show host Rush Limbaugh, and I turned up the volume. At one point, Letterman asked with his characteristic wry wit, "Rush, do you ever wake up in the middle of the night and think to yourself, 'Boy, I'm full of a whole lot of hot air'?"

Limbaugh responded quickly: "No."

Whether Rush was kidding or not, I do not know. But I do know that many of us spend our lives trying to convince others that we have it all together. In contrast, the joyful Christian life begins with the admission that we are full of a whole lot of hot air, and we need a great deal of help. There is incredible freedom in admitting this. In facing our own failures and moving on. We are, each of us, fragile creatures, whose hope does not lie in our own goodness or ability, but in the fact that Christ died for our sin and that God can take our weaknesses and use them.

Friedrich Nietzsche, the famous German philosopher, gave up on Christianity not because of a lack of evidence but because of a lack of a role model who was real and full of grace. Nietzsche once wrote of his father, who was a pastor, "Does that thing up there ever laugh or cry? Does he ever feel anything? Does what he preaches ever find itself in real human experience?"

Thomas Jefferson called honesty "the first chapter in the book of wisdom," and Charles Swindoll once said these very wise words: "Honesty has a beautiful and refreshing simplicity about it. No ulterior motives. No hidden meanings. An absence of hypocrisy, duplicity, political games, and verbal superficiality. As honesty and real integrity characterize our lives, there will be no need to manipulate others."

What does it mean to get real?

It means that pretending is no longer in our bag of tricks. That we have accepted the reality that we are sinners, that nothing we do will impress God. As a result, all that we do comes not from guilt or obligation, but from thanksgiving for all that God has done.

Jesus could rest, not because the future was friendly—He knew what awaited Him on the cross—but because He had gone about His Father's business, He had been faithful today. You and I, too, are capable of this much.

In the next few pages I'd like you to meet four amazing individuals who bring this truth to life. A few are missionary friends of mine. One is a singer. And the fourth is an ordinary guy who changed my world.

39

Doug's Last Wish

We say we must do all we can.
Jesus says we must let God do all we can.
—OSWALD CHAMBERS

Over the years it has been my privilege to interview hundreds of people for magazine articles and books. Some are missionaries, others are wealthy financiers, and many are well-known celebrities. I suppose if I had to separate them into two categories, there would be the stars and there would be the servants. Please don't ask me for a list of names. Two of those humble servants recently sat down with our family for a meal of roast beef and all the trimmings. Our children are happiest when there is good food, good stories, and plenty of dessert. This evening offered all three.

Doug and Margaret Nichols have faced their share of obstacles. After surgery for colon cancer in April 1993, Doug sat across from his doctor and listened in disbelief. "I'm sorry, Doug," said the doctor nervously, "but you do have a 30 percent chance of recovery."

"You mean I have a 70 percent chance of dying?" asked Doug, with a grin.

"I wouldn't put it that way," said a surprised doctor. "But my best estimate is that you have about three months to live."

228

"Well, let me tell you something, Doc," said Nichols, "Whatever happens, I have a 100 percent chance of going to heaven."

One year later radiation and chemo treatments had left Doug's body wracked with pain. Though he kept his humor well-oiled, both Doug and Margaret knew the end might be near. But their world was not the only one collapsing. Nightly news reports from Rwanda indicated that civil war had spiraled out of control and more than a million people had been slaughtered, many by their own neighbors and trusted friends. The carnage was beyond belief. Terrified Rwandans by the thousands had fled across the border into Zaire and crowded into filthy, ill-equipped refugee camps, where diseases such as cholera found a ready home. People were dying everywhere—50,000 in three days alone in the little town of Goma. As Margaret and Doug read the terrible accounts and saw the images on TV, their hearts were broken. But what could one couple do?

"I knew I was going to die," Doug told me, "but I wanted to do something before leaving this earth. I just wanted to hold some of those children in my arms and try to offer hope."

Soon Doug found himself traveling with a team of doctors and nurses through the heart of Rwanda, with no idea of the adventure that lay ahead.

A Rwandan Christian leader whom Doug had worked with before had hired 300 refugees as stretcher bearers to bury the daily masses of dead and transport the sick so doctors could do their best. One day the leader approached Doug with an expression of deep concern. "Mr. Nichols," he said, "we have a problem."

"What is it?" Doug asked.

"I was given only so much money to hire these people, and now they want to go on strike."

"What? In the middle of all this death and destruction these men want to go on strike?"

"They want more money."

"But we have no more money," Doug informed him. "We've spent everything. If they don't work, thousands will die."

His friend shrugged his shoulders. "They're not going to work. They want more money."

"Well, can I talk to them?"

"It won't do any good. They're angry. Who knows what they'll do?"

Finally Doug's friend agreed. Walking over to an old burned-out school building, Doug climbed the steps wondering what on earth he could say. Three hundred angry men surrounded the Rwandan who would act as interpreter. "Mr. Nichols wants to say something," he called above the clamor as Doug desperately searched for words that would get through to them.

"I can't possibly understand the pain you've experienced," Doug began, "and now, seeing your wives and children dying from cholera, I can never understand how that feels. Maybe you want more money for food and water and medical supplies for your families. I've never been in that position either. Nothing tragic has ever happened in my life that compares to what you've suffered. The only thing that's ever happened to me is that I've got cancer."

He was about to go on when the interpreter stopped. "Excuse me," he said, "did you say *cancer?*"

"Yes."

"And you came over here? Did your doctor say you could come?"

"He told me that if I came to Africa I'd probably be dead in three days."

"Your doctor told you that and you still came? What did you come for? And what if you die?"

"I'm here because God led us to come and do something for these people in His name," Doug told him. "I'm no hero. If I die, just bury me out in that field where you bury everybody else."

To Doug's utter amazement the man began to weep. Then, with tears flowing down his face, he turned back to the workers and began to preach. "This man has cancer," he told the crowd, which suddenly grew very quiet. In Rwanda, cancer is an automatic death sentence. "He came over here willing to die for our people," the interpreter continued, "and we're going on strike just to get a little bit more money? We should be ashamed!"

Suddenly men on all sides began falling to their knees in tears. Doug had no idea what was going on because no one had bothered to translate. To his great embarrassment, one fellow crawled over and threw his arms around Doug's legs. Dumbfounded, Doug watched as people stood to their feet, walked over to their stretchers, and went quietly back to work.

Later, as the interpreter recounted the whole story, Doug thought to himself, *What did I do? Nothing. It wasn't my ability to care for the sick. It wasn't my ability to organize. All I did was get cancer. But God used that very weakness to move the hearts of people.* Because they went back to work, thousands of lives were saved, and many heard the good news of Jesus Christ.

"So many are discouraged by weakness," Doug told me later. "We feel that God could never use us; we have nothing to offer. But you can get sick, can't you? You can simply obey God and do what He calls you to do—whether you feel you have the ability to do the job or not. Sickness and weakness—those things we think God cannot use—are many times the exact things God uses to glorify His name. But so often much is left undone in the world because we are so concerned about what people will think about us. We are underqualified; we've never done that before. And so we sit back as spectators."

It has been my privilege to meet many learned people through the years, but those who have had the most profound effect on my life are the relatively unlettered ones like Doug who are too "underqualified" to ever take the credit when good things happen. Over roast beef and all the trimmings, my children listened wide-eared, as Doug told us another story.

When he and Margaret were working in Manila with the organization Action International, they were asked to begin a ministry among street children in Calcutta similar to what they were doing in the Philippines. Doug traveled to India for two weeks to survey the situation and then prepared for his return to Manila by way of Bangkok. Emotionally drained and exhausted from the heat and the filth and the poverty of Calcutta, he could hardly wait to board that beautiful Thai airliner with orchids pinned to the seat, fresh orange juice, and air-conditioning. As he basked in the cleanliness and freshness of the big jumbo jet, Doug looked over and noticed that the entire center section was empty. "When the plane takes off," he thought, "I'm heading over there to stretch out and sleep all the way to Bangkok." He could hardly wait.

Minutes before the scheduled departure, a steady stream of people entered the cabin carrying large woven baskets. They set a basket in each seat, five seats across, until the entire center section was full. Curiosity got the better of Doug, so he undid his seat belt and stood up to see what was in the baskets. Babies. Two in every basket. There must have been close to a hundred, all orphans headed to Bangkok and then on to Germany for adoption. And there were only two Indian women to take care of all those children. As Doug sat down again, he knew there would be no sleep on this plane.

The flight attendant was beginning her check as they sped down the runway toward takeoff when all of a sudden she looked over at all these babies and became very alarmed. She ran to one of the Indian women and began chattering excitedly in Thai. The young woman didn't understand Thai, and the more she didn't understand the more excited the flight attendant became. The attendant began yelling and scared the young woman, who burst out in tears. Once again Doug got up from his seat, this time to see what was the matter, and discovered the problem—the baskets weren't buckled in.

"I don't know much," Doug told our kids, "but I can buckle a seat belt." Reaching over, he fastened the belt over a basket. Then he went to the next one, buckled it, and went to the next one, row after row. The plane was gathering speed, and as he secured the last basket, jumped into his seat, and buckled his own seat belt, the plane lifted off.

"Wow," said the fellow next to him as he caught his breath, "you must really like babies!"

"No," Doug laughed, "not particularly."

"Then why did you do that?"

He thought for a moment before answering. Then he told him bluntly, "Sir, it's like this. I did it because I didn't want to sin."

The man turned to Doug with a questioning glance. "What does buckling in babies have to do with sin?"

"Well," said Doug, who never misses an opening, "I'm a Christian, and I try to live the way God asks me to in His Word, the Bible. It tells us how to know Him personally and how to obey Him as we live this life. There's a verse that says, 'Anyone, then, who knows the good thing he ought to do and doesn't do it, sins.'"

The man stared at him, incredulously. "Are you sure that's in the Bible?"

"I sure hope so," said Doug, as he opened his New Testament and showed him James 4:17.

"Wow!" the man said again.

Just as Doug suspected, he never did get to sleep, but that was alright. "I was able to share the glorious gospel of Christ with my homosexual seatmate all the way to Bangkok," he smiles. "I'm no evangelist, but God is not hindered by our weakness or lack of resources."

My children were still listening.

"You might not be able to do much either, kids, but can you get sick? Can you buckle in babies?"

They nodded their heads.

For me, Doug and Margaret's lives are living illustrations that God only requires what we can give Him. He doesn't ask that we serve Him in misery, but with joy, doing what we can. Never forgetting Who gets the credit.

40

Tyranny of the Insignificant

*God can make you anything you want to be, but
you have to put everything in his hands.*
—Mahalia Jackson (1911–1972)

On the evening of December 31, 1999, Barbra Streisand rang in the new millenium at the MGM Grand in Las Vegas, Nevada, taking home $13 million for her efforts. Streisand shipped furniture, rugs, and paintings from her home in Los Angeles to ensure a "homey" atmosphere. She also demanded that the theater seats be replaced and the room reinsulated to provide acoustics better suited to her voice. I told this to veteran singer/songwriter Wayne Watson recently, and he simply laughed. "I had some pretty amazing offers back then," he recalls, "but I was home with my family that night. We were out in the backyard watching neighbors shoot off fireworks."

It was a fitting conclusion to one of the most bittersweet years of Wayne's life.

In January, during a family ski trip to Colorado, Wayne took a wrong turn, careening downhill and breaking several bones in his body. "I was forced out of the game for three or four months," he recalls. "Pneumonia set in. I broke a rib coughing. It took me until August to get back on my feet, and a year later I was still feeling repercussions. I didn't know if I'd ever leave my room again, much less write another song or do another concert."

As Wayne lay in bed on a forced sabbatical, he couldn't have known that God was orchestrating another story a thousand miles away. One that would intersect his in a most remarkable way.

By the time Martha Williamson became a Christian in 1981, she was already a trusted associate producer in Hollywood. Soon "the Jesus girl," as her associates dubbed her, began praying that God would perform a miracle in Tinseltown. But the dream looked impossible. Hollywood, she knew, is synonymous with money. And projects with Christian messages don't sell. But when Martha was invited to become executive producer of a television show called *Angel's Attic,* she wondered if the dream was coming true. As she watched the tape, however, discouragement set in. The angels quarreled. And worse, their Boss stood in direct opposition to the God she had come to know and love. Dialing the vice president of the network, she told him, "I'm sorry. I know you've invested a lot in this show. But it's just not the kind of thing I want to do."

"But that's why we sent it to you, Martha," he replied. "It needs to be turned into the type of program you and other talented people *will* want to do."

Martha met with the executives and boldly told them, "Angels...are messengers of God, and they do what He says. The show shouldn't be about the angels, but about whether the people the angels appear to are willing to do what God wants. That's where the drama is. And we need to confront the big questions: Why did God let my baby die? Where is God in the midst of terminal illness? Why doesn't God stop evil people from victimizing the defenseless?"

"Can we take on issues like that?" the executives asked.

"We have to," she replied, "and we can do it from the standpoint that God loves everyone and wants the best for them; that He's intervening through angelic messengers so that our characters, who are in critical situations, will know He loves them and then do the right thing."

"Can you reshoot some scenes and adapt the original pilot?"

"No."

Shock registered on their faces as they tried to swallow a $2 million loss. "Why don't you wait next door for a few minutes," suggested the president.

Calling Martha back to the meeting, he said, "We want you to do everything you just said. But we need the first episode in three weeks. As of right now you've got an office and a parking space, and you'd better get started. Deal?"

The result of the deal was the enormously popular show *Touched by an Angel*.

One day, as Martha pulled out of a parking lot, a voice from her car radio caused her to stop and listen. It was Wayne Watson's voice. The song was "For Such a Time As This," Wayne's call to be faithful and holy, to shine, lighting up the darkness.

The song would be the perfect backdrop for the next episode of her show.

"Martha told me later that she never listens to the car radio," Wayne Watson told me, "but one of her children had left it on. That's how it all got started." The original plan was to have Bette Midler record the song, but when they finally asked Wayne how he would feel if his version was used, he thought for a split second, then laughed. "That's okay," he said. "I think I can handle that."

The September season premiere was named after Wayne's song "For Such a Time As This."

"In a matter of five minutes, 20 million people heard that song," says Wayne, in amazement. "I haven't played to that many people in my life. In 20 years of singing, this has been the highlight, something that I didn't orchestrate at all. Something that took place while I was flat on my back."

Though he wouldn't have chosen it, good things have grown from difficulty in Wayne's life. His ever-popular song "When God's People Pray" was written at a time when his best friend's wife was ill with leukemia. "We believed prayer was integral in her living as long as she did and that God answered prayer whether it went our way or not," he says.

In a fast-forward industry that is notorious for ripping families apart, Watson and his wife have just celebrated their twenty-fifth wedding anniversary.

> I am so thankful. We married at 19 and the statistics were against us. The divorce rate for people who marry under the age of 25 is twice as high as for people who marry over 25. I was barely 19. But we went into it with the support and example of godly parents and the belief that divorce wasn't an option. I'm saddened when my friends are divorced. But I'm a realist. I look at life the way it is, not the way it should be. We have to be on guard. Whenever we start thinking we're above some sin or failure, we need to live with the awareness that we're always one bad decision from disaster. I could walk out of here today and do something that would ruin my marriage, ruin my family, and cost me the respect of my sons—a respect that would never be recovered. I've had people in this industry who have failed miserably tell me, "Wayne, I didn't get away with anything—the pain I have borne is more than you'll

ever know." They're devastated and they will never be the same.

Wayne has received worldwide fame for his 14 albums, 20 number one songs, a Grammy nomination, and numerous Dove Awards, yet he is quick to say that he has learned more from four months in the valley than many years on the mountaintop:

> Dave Dravecky, the pitcher who lost his arm to cancer, told me that the mountaintop is a great place to breath clean fresh air and have a good view, but nothing grows on the top of mountains. If you want to grow you've got to go down where the dirt is, in the valley. I don't like growth. It hurts. God said He wouldn't forsake us, but He didn't say He wouldn't break us. Real growth comes when we reach a point where Christ is our rest and our only shelter.
>
> I learned that the sun kept coming up whether I had a new album out or not. Over 20 years I've never really taken any extended time off. But when I did, I found that no one was standing at my door threatening to throw me out of the house. It makes me wonder why I was killing myself so much all those years. The pace we set for ourselves sometimes is not very realistic and it's not very healthy. Sometimes it's a good idea to ask ourselves, "Am I too easily occupied with the urgency of the insignificant?"
>
> Who knows what God is orchestrating next? But what gives me hope is that God is bigger than my comprehension. All of my thinking and analyzing and theorizing about theology and the world at large is just the tip of the iceberg. There's

so much about God I don't understand. Faith requires trust in something I don't see or something I don't get. I visualize God picking me and my family up, and while the world speeds up and people reach in to try and rip us apart, He's got us under the protection of His mighty arm. And we can sit there quietly and safely, trusting Him whether we understand it all or not.

41

Howard's Beginning

The man who surrenders to Christ exchanges a
cruel slave driver for a kind and gentle Master
whose yoke is easy and whose burden is light.
—A.W. Tozer

Night falls quickly on the highlands of Ethiopia, causing
the horizon to vanish in a gray mist. At 9600 feet the air
turns bitter cold, and the twisted laughter of wild hyenas
echoing below cuts the darkness. The young missionary
shivers as he crawls into his hastily assembled wooden
shelter, wraps himself in a thin sleeping bag, and wonders
again, *What on earth am I doing here? I could be back in
America sipping coffee, watching the Lakers.*

From nearby villages the sound of singing and dancing
blends with the mesmerizing beat of drums. A spiritual darkness seems to blanket the hills, making the young man's mission seem less and less possible.

Since he was a child, Howard Brant has dreamed of telling
these people about God's love for them. But now he wonders: How will the good news of Jesus ever penetrate such
inky blackness? Can it possibly reach through the occult
worship, the pagan rituals of a hardened culture? Through a
crack in the shelter he spies a faint star, high in the night sky.

An hour ago the star was invisible.

It took the darkness to bring it out.

241

"Lord," Howard prays, "I feel like that star up there. A little light surrounded by a great darkness. That's me. There's nobody else here who knows about Jesus. I feel so alone." Then a voice seems to say, "I am the One who put that star there, Howard. I put it there to show you that in all this darkness, one tiny light can make an enormous difference."

Can it really? Howard falls asleep wondering.

As a student at Prairie Bible College in Canada, Howard Brant was determined to take the good news of Christ to Africa—just as his parents had done. He had grown up in Ethiopia, and when his wife, Jo-Ann, and he set foot once again on Ethiopian soil, it was like coming home.

Elated to be appointed principal of a Bible school at the mission station of Woliso, Howard almost popped some buttons thinking about it. Me! Principal of a school! But he arrived to discover that the student body consisted of a grand total of three students. Though he learned a lesson in humility, Howard was undaunted. "Let's go preach up in the mountains," he told the three, "and see if God will increase the enrollment." Sure enough, within a few weeks, 18 students had joined the school.

They listened respectfully as Howard began teaching them how to preach—just the way he had learned. "One man gave his message," remembers Howard with a laugh, "complete with three points and a poem. Then he said, 'That's what Mr. Howie wanted me to say. Now I will tell you what I'd like to say...' So the students really taught the teacher. I learned to teach God's Word in the context of their lives and their culture."

One step was the closing of school on Thursdays—something I wish my teachers would have done more often. But Howard's purpose was to give the students an assignment: "Go out in twos or threes and share your faith. Every time you hear a question, write it down."

When the students returned, they handed in their note-books. On weekends, Howard pored over the questions, and they became the basis for the school's curriculum.

One day the students returned, excited. "We've found a group of people in the mountains. They've never heard of Jesus." Sure enough, nearly three-quarters of a million people—the Gurage—lived nearby. Firing off a letter to mission headquarters in Addis Ababa, Howard bluntly reminded them that these people were dying without any knowledge of the One who could save them. Unless they did something to reach these people, they would be responsible to God!

So the mission did something.

They sent Howard.

That night beneath the faint star was the first night of Howard's first expedition. "My plan is bigger than yours, Howard," God seemed to be saying. "You just hang on and watch."

Jo-Ann soon joined him in a tiny village, and together they built a small school and medical clinic. One day Howard looked up and saw a local judge coming down the path toward him. "Sir," Howard said, "I would love to teach you about the Lord Jesus."

"I've been thinking about that, and I want to talk to you," the man replied. Howard couldn't believe his ears. "My boy comes to your school," the man continued, "and every night I ask him questions about what you teach him."

Before long the judge became the first believer in the area, and soon he was teaching others. Within months there were six little clusters of believers there in the mountains.

But the darkness descended often. Girls walking down a path would suddenly fall over, barely able to move. Carried to the hut of the fetish leader, they would speak in a language they had never used before. Back in their own village, when-ever the cult leaders walked past, the girls would suddenly grow wild-eyed and convulsive and run from their homes to follow them back into the forest.

"As we began to preach about the miracles of Jesus," remembers Howard, "many were miraculously delivered." When the cult leader appeared and those women who had been possessed sat peacefully, everyone was astounded at the power of God, and the word began to spread.

One morning when Howard turned on the radio, the ominous sound of drums and martial music filled the air. The revolution had begun. Emperor Haile Selassie had been deposed, and the Communists had taken over. "I thought about what had happened in other countries when this happened," says Howard, "and I considered running. Then the words of John 10 came to me, how the hired hand flees because he cares nothing for the sheep but the good shepherd stays out of love, even laying down his life. I knew we couldn't desert our new believers. Their faith was about to be tested. We must stay, regardless of the cost."

Agonizing over how best to use the remaining time, Howard concluded that he should invest in a few believers who would be able to teach others after his wife and he were either forced out or killed. While studying John 17 one night, he noticed that God gave Jesus specific individuals to disciple. Finding several believers, Howard told them, "If you want me to teach you about Jesus, come to my hut tomorrow when the sun reaches straight overhead. I will take the first six who come."

The next morning Howard waited. Three men arrived: the judge, an older man who was strong in faith, and a younger man. Exactly the ones Howard would have chosen. The sun rose higher. Would there be more?

Late in the morning two strangers approached. "We want to be taught about God," they said.

"Are you Christians?" asked Howard.

They shook their heads.

"But a disciple must be a Christian," said Howard.

They shrugged.

"We heard that you teach people about God, so we decided to come."

Howard thought of the New Testament disciples when they first met Jesus. Did they understand that He was the Son of God? Or did they just follow, believing in the process? Standing to his feet, he invited the strangers in.

It was almost noon when he heard a nervous cough and looked outside. There stood Balaynesh, a woman with a twisted spine. "I would like to be a disciple," she said, shyly.

"You don't understand," said Howard, "I'm...well...I'm not looking for a woman. I need men, strong men, who can trek with me through the mountains, teaching and preaching." Howard knew she wouldn't last a day. Holding his Bible in front of her, he asked, "Can you read?"

"No," she replied, "I've only had grade one." Then Balaynesh looked at him with big brown eyes. "Please?"

"God seemed to be saying to me, 'Howard, you asked for six. You've got six.'" Howard smiled, and welcomed her in.

Within days the seven of them were trudging through the mountains, visiting huts, attending funerals, sleeping on dusty floors, eating whatever was available. All the while, they were teaching by example—washing feet, listening to problems, giving medical help.

But their deeds didn't go unnoticed by the Communists. The Communists began turning students and teachers against the small band, stealing their car and their belongings. One day while Howard was gone, 26 armed soldiers searched his house and terrorized his family. "When I arrived home," he recalls, "they let my family go, but placed me under house arrest."

Locked in his own home, Howard was thankful that his captors allowed him visitors. The six joined him daily for a rather intense discipleship program.

One day he was given the word. You are free to go, but you must leave the country.

A world away, Howard and Jo-Ann prayed for the six disciples. They prayed that God would work in their absence. Eight years passed, and finally Howard was permitted to return to Ethiopia and travel to a distant part of the country. What the Communist government didn't know was that the Gurage Mountains were right in his path. Reaching them by nightfall, Howard parked his car and took off into the hills and valleys he knew so well. The tribe sent out runners, and believers began to gather. Joyfully he greeted the little band of four disciples.

"When you left," they told him, "we felt abandoned. But finally we decided to go out preaching like we did when you were with us."

"How many churches are there?" asked Howard.

"We don't have churches," they replied. "The Communists have closed them all. We meet in houses."

"How many believers are here?" asked Howard, dreading their reply.

"We have no idea," they responded. "Five thousand. Eight thousand."

Howard's eyes lit up with astonishment. "Who led all these people to Jesus?" he asked.

They grinned at him. They shrugged their shoulders. "We did," they replied.

All of them had been in prison.

"Where are the other two?" asked Howard, bracing himself for their reply. They took him to the grave of one who died a martyr behind bars.

"And where...where is Balaynesh?" he asked.

"She can't come," one of them answered. "Two thousand women are meeting secretly for a conference, and she's the main teacher. She's the leader of all the women in the tribe."

Howard remembered the time when he had asked the crippled woman if she could read. She'll never last a day, he had thought. How wrong he was. The torch had been passed. The light was shining, brighter than ever.

42

Squeeze the Day

*The men who are lifting the world upward
and onward are those who encourage
more than criticize.*
—ELIZABETH HARRISON

Two major events took place during the week this book
was due. First of all, I turned 40. Don't worry, I am not
having a midlife crisis yet. I will wait to finish this chapter
before I dye my hair. Several birthday cards arrived from
friends who were trying to be helpful, I'm sure. One contained a bumper sticker that said, "Forty's not old. For an
oak tree." I also received enough Grecian Formula to outfit
the Golden Hills Lodge. And Preparation H, a cane, suspenders, and calcium pills. Gord and Joanne Robideau,
former friends of mine, sent me the following note:

Dear Phil,

Because of the advancing age now upon you, we
thought we would help you out with some new
book ideas to appeal to your aging audience. Perhaps it is time to consider a new direction for
your pen. Here are the ideas. You may keep the
royalties all to yourself.

Honey, I Blew Up the Balloon and Got Winded

Who Put My Bifocals in the Fridge?

Making Life Rich Without Any Hair

Honey, I Forgot the Kids' Names

I Used to Have Answers, Now I Can't Remember the Questions

I Used to Play Hockey, Now I Have Arthritis

Who Put the Wrinkles in My Cheeks?

After my fortieth birthday party, my eldest son said, "Don't worry, Dad. They're working on a cure for old age, you know."

At their worst, birthdays are an odometer, a depressing reminder of how fast life flies. At their best, they provide a milestone, reminding us to celebrate another year, to give thanks for the gift of life, to follow the psalmist's advice and "consider how short our lives really are so that we may be wise."

Our entire community has been considering such things this week.

On Sunday night I returned from a trip and noticed that the customary sparkle in my wife's eyes had been replaced by sadness. "I have bad news," she said, putting an arm around me. "Cordell is gone. Killed in a car accident."

I slumped to the floor in disbelief. "No," was all I could manage. My friend. One of my biggest encouragers. Gone. It couldn't be.

On Friday morning the thirteenth of July, I had talked with him.

"This is the happiest day of my life," he had said. "I've given the family business over to my son. I'm ready for the next step." A few hours later he had taken that step—into the presence of God.

The world slows down remarkably when a friend dies. Things you once thought important don't mean a thing. Things you worried about yesterday vanish today. Money won't buy what you want, and sometimes you find yourself wishing for five more minutes to say what you didn't say when you knew you should have.

On the weekend, Kathy Friesen, a longtime family friend, had told me the story of a small dog, abandoned by someone on a country road when Kathy was a little girl. The dog took up residence near the church Kathy's family attended, and each Sunday it waddled through the parking lot, warmly greeting everyone who arrived. "It didn't jump all over us," smiled Kathy, "just wagged its tail, as if to say, 'Good to see you...what took you so long to come back?'"

Cordell did that at our church. He didn't leave things unsaid. He met you in the foyer with welcome written on his face and encouragement all over his lips. Some people have been bitten in church parking lots. Never by Cordell. Some consider it their spiritual gift to complain about the music, or the hairdos, or the sermon. Cordell told you how wonderful things were. Some delight in pointing fingers at the world. Cordell told you what God was doing there. "Awesome" was one of his favorite words. "Fabulous" was another. Though he was 20 years my senior, he called me Uncle Phil.

A few days after his death, I found myself stopping to talk to children, adopting Cordell's vocabulary, encouraging people I should have encouraged long ago.

Sometimes you can measure a man's influence by the volume of cigarette butts in the church parking lot at his funeral. There were plenty at this one. Fifteen hundred people don't show up to much in a small town, but they gathered to say goodbye today. Many were "pre-Christians," as Cordell liked to call them. Dozens considered him their best friend. As a member of what the insurance world calls the Million Dollar Round Table, Cordell had worked hard and experienced much of what we term success. But he always seemed to have time for people. Teenagers in our town called him their mentor. He was my high school hockey coach, my cheerleader, and one of my biggest fans. He climbed so high because he helped others up.

"Who makes a humorist laugh?" someone once asked me. "Guys like Cordell," I replied. "My father was part Scotch," he had jokingly told me over a glass of Pepsi a week before his death, "part ginger ale."

This morning as we left for the funeral, I told my sons I would pay them a dime for every adjective they wrote down that was used to describe Cordell. Their pockets are jingling tonight. "He loved God and he loved baseball," wrote my son Stephen. Comforter. Encourager. Servant. He was honest in business. He enjoyed life. Cordell had the ability to make you think you were his best friend even if he'd just met you. "He invited us over to watch the World Series," said Stephen. "He kept filling my glass with Pepsi and he got me more chips."

When my wife and I were first married, Cordell took us out for lunch, hoping to sell us life insurance. And he told us that no matter what our decision, the very best life insurance policy wasn't for sale. The assurance that we can live forever with Jesus by simple faith in God is the best present we'll ever receive, and it's free for the asking. It is a message that has changed our lives.

Hours before Cordell's death I spent some time on the phone with one of my favorite authors, Philip Yancey. He was talking about people who have increased his faith and helped him survive hypocrisy in the church. We compared notes a little. Our backgrounds have similarities, yet both of us find ourselves drawn to the church like moths to a flame. Sometimes we experience the light. And sometimes we get burned. But certain ones along the way keep bringing us back. They are the tail-waggers. People like Cordell.

I wish for every church a Cordell. For every community and every home. If something blessed him, he said so. He was human like the rest of us, but he kept pointing us higher. Cordell couldn't sing to save his life, nor could he change a lightbulb. But he could light up your face with a compliment. He never met anyone who was just plain ordinary. They were fantastic, unbelievable, or incredible. Cordell liked to catch people doing something right, and praise them for it! Cordell used exclamation marks when he described you. He looked past my faults and embellished my attributes. I picture him walking around heaven now, patting angels between the wings, saying, "Wow! Good job! You're amazing! You've been doing this how many years?"

A few months ago Cordell sat in my office, struggling to balance a busy schedule with God's will. He was tired. Worn out. He laughed when I told him the topic of the book I was writing, and he thanked me for making him laugh late at night while he read my others.

"We've confused successfulness with fruitfulness," said Cordell, staring out my third-story window. "Success brings some rewards and maybe even fame. But real joy comes from being fruitful."

I nodded and thought about his words.

"I'm learning to slow down," he said, smiling. "To squeeze the day. Six grandchildren help you do that."

"Let's get together soon," were Cordell's last words to me.

One day soon I'll keep that appointment. I can hardly wait.

43

The Last Chapter

It is since Christians have largely ceased to think of the other world that they have become so ineffective in this [one].
—C.S. Lewis (1898–1963)

Just days before his execution, mass murderer Timothy McVey was quoted in our local newspaper as saying, "I don't believe in God or in hell...but if I end up there I'll have plenty of company." Infamous last words, and a startling reminder that our view of the next world dramatically impacts how we live in this one.

The hope of heaven should bring balance to our busy lives, reminding us to neglect the insignificant and to remember that we are leaving footprints everywhere we go.

On Friday my aging parents bought a brand new stereo because they could no longer hear the old one. The old one was an attractive little unit, complete with record player and 8-track, the same model Noah used on the Ark when he wanted a weather report. I was explaining to Mom and Dad how to set the digital clock and what an equalizer was for, when my son Jeffrey, who had been admiring the flashing lights and the 100-watt speakers, said, "Um, Grandpa, you should put this thing in your will. I'd kinda like it. You're not gonna live much longer anyway."

Thank goodness my 78-year-old father is rather hard of hearing, so he said, "Bill? Who's Bill?"

I was chewing a large mint at the time, and it became lodged in my throat, causing Jeffrey to practice Mr. Heimlich's maneuver, one of the useful things he is learning in sixth grade.

My mother laughed until she almost fell off her rocking chair, then recovered enough to say, "Well, Jeffrey, the Bible says it's good to remember how short our lives are, 'so that we may be wise.'"

"Surprise? What surprise?" said Dad, causing me to swallow the remaining mint altogether.

That night at the dinner table I waited until my wife was halfway through a carrot, then recounted the incident. My timing was poor, but the laughter was plentiful.

Dinnertime is the one hour of the day when our five schedules intersect. When possible, we clear appointments, brew tea, and linger long on dessert—whatever it takes to keep the conversation going.

Tonight while we eat unheated S'mores, I pull out a file long forgotten. The label says "Kids—Funny Stuff." It includes things done and said in our children's younger years. The first item is rather cute. When Rachael was four, she forgot to put her Sunday school offering in the plate. "Uh, oh," she said on the way home, "I forgot to pay the teacher." On a Sunday evening when Stephen was five, we were talking about heaven. I could tell the boy was thinking hard. "When you die," he said finally, "do they take you to the body shop?" Driving by a cemetery one day, this same child noticed a grave being dug and said, "Dad, look! One got out!" A year ago, Jeffrey asked Grandpa, "How old are you?" Jeffrey's eyes grew wide at the answer. "Wow," he said, "you must be getting ready for heaven."

We've been talking more about heaven lately, partly because I just turned 40, but also because kids aren't afraid to talk of such things. Those who think about heaven aren't running away from life, they're running toward it.

"I don't wanna go to heaven," says Jeffrey, who is too young not to be honest.

"Um...why do say that, son?"

"Well, all we're gonna do is sit around and talk."

"Where did you hear that?"

"Well, that's all you grown-ups do. I heard we're just gonna worship God all the time. With a worship band and stuff."

"Yeah," chimes in Rachael. "And there won't be dogs in heaven. If Mojo won't be there, I don't wanna go either."

"The Bible doesn't say dogs won't be in heaven," I interject. "Just cats."

Rachael wraps me on the knuckles with her spoon.

Later that night, the kids come one at a time into our bedroom. Next to dinner, this is the best time for talking, it seems. The dog sprawls on the bed, dreaming of something we'll never know. Kids surround us, and the conversation turns once again to heaven.

"I won't be going to heaven because I've written books or spoken to huge crowds of people," I tell them. "Or because I've been a good boy." My wife rolls her eyes and laughs. "You're not kidding," she says.

"I'll be there because Christ died on the cross and rose again. All I did was accept the gift. All I had to do was receive Him."

"One thing I'm gonna like about heaven is the fruit," says Rachael. "There'll be tons of fruit in heaven."

A thought hits me. "Rachael, what books are you reading?"

"The Chronicles of Narnia."

"Go and get book seven, would you?"

Moments later I am flipping through *The Last Battle*. "I hate to give away the ending, you guys, but the children all die. That's life you know. But death is not the end of the story. Listen to the last paragraph:

> But the things that began to happen after that were so great and beautiful that I cannot write them. And...we can most truly say that they all lived happily ever after. But for them it was only the beginning of the real story. All their life in this world and all their adventures in Narnia had only been the cover and the title page: now at last they were beginning chapter one of the great story which no one on earth has read: which goes on forever: in which every chapter is better than the one before.

"I wish I had more answers about heaven," I say. "I hope there's golf and chocolate and green grass and colors we haven't seen yet. But Jesus will be there, and you will be too, so it's gonna be out of this world."

The kids are quiet now. The dog is stirring. I pat its head. "Will there be stereos in heaven?" Jeffrey interrupts our thoughts.

"Not the kind we have here," I answer.

"Good," says Jeffrey, grinning widely. "Then Grandpa won't be needing his."

44

The Speed of Grace

*Excessive activism is typical of those
who do not live by grace.*
—CHARLES BRUTSCH

More than 60 years ago, my father served with the Canadian Armed Forces in World War II. A few months ago, I asked Mom if I could see some of the correspondence and clippings surrounding that turbulent period of their lives. Sitting quietly in the living room, I examined the contents of a tiny scrapbook containing black and white photos—some crystal clear, some badly faded—and letters from my mom's older brother, my Uncle Lorne.

"When he was a small boy," Mother said, smiling, "Lorne used to tell me, 'If you ever feel like you're dying, just keep running. As long as you keep running, your heart keeps beating and you can't die.'"

At the age of 24, Lorne found himself running through Europe, dodging Nazi bullets, fighting for the liberation of France. In a handwritten letter postmarked August 30, 1944, he wrote these words:

Dear Mother and Dad,

We are still going strong and every day sees us closer to home. There are several things you must get used to here—to know the sound of your own guns from the enemy, to take discomfort as it comes and also to admit that you have been scared. It is funny how a few days ago we were diving into our slit trenches. When the danger was past, we came out and laughed at each other's fantastic jumps to safety. You must look at the lighter side of life here, for I've seen those who tried to restrain themselves give in to a case of bad nerves. War makes you think of many different things and all in the space of a minute. You might laugh, joke and pray all inside those 60 seconds and when it is all over you say, "Well, that wasn't so bad. I feel ready for more." During the last few days I've seen the real reason we are here. I've been greeted by these French people and the greeting is sincere. They have told their children of us, from the smallest to the biggest for they too wave and run to clasp your hand. A candy in their hand and you are a friend for life. One day soon it will be over and we'll all go to our homes. Keep smiling Mom and Dad, and keep praying for us over here. One day soon we'll all be round that table again, talking over the years gone by.

Love to you all,

Lorne

It was his last letter home. Seven days later Lorne was shot and killed by a sniper's bullet.

Each year on November 11, we Canadians gather for Remembrance Day with services and memorials intended to celebrate our freedom. But increasingly, as the veterans move on, it seems easy for my generation to forget the incredible sacrifice millions of men and women made that we might be free.

With that in mind, my wife and I finally summoned the courage to watch *Saving Private Ryan*, Steven Spielberg's haunting window on the days surrounding the Allied invasion at Omaha Beach. When the film was first released, war veterans broke down in theaters, many unable to process the memories invoked by the soldier's-eye view of the horrors of battle. I don't blame them. I sat with my trigger finger on the remote control's "fast-forward" button during the first 30 minutes. And I must confess to covering my eyes with a pillow on two occasions.

When the scene finally switches from the bloody beaches to a peaceful America, we see a mother glancing up from her sink as a U.S. army car creeps up the dusty driveway and stops before her farmhouse. Ever since her four sons had enlisted, in hopes of halting Hitler's bloody advance, she has been praying this moment would never come. One of her boys is gone, she realizes in horror. Which one could it be? But the news is worse than she could have imagined.

That day she is handed not one, but three telegrams. Three of her four boys are dead. And the fourth is missing.

Sinking to her knees on the porch, she watches the dishtowel slip from her trembling hands.

Stirred by the grief-stricken woman's plight, the U.S. Army chief of staff, General George C. Marshall, resorts to unusual measures. He orders Captain John Miller (Tom Hanks), a hero of the Omaha Beach battle, to lead eight men across the picturesque French countryside to find the fourth son, paratrooper Private James Ryan. His mission: Bring Ryan home alive. Together they strike out, heading in the general direction of Cherbourg. Though their mission is eventually accomplished, the cost is high. Most of the eight lose their lives, and in an act of the ultimate sacrifice, Captain Miller gives his own life to save Private Ryan.

The film concludes in modern-day France as an aging war veteran shuffles up to a grave in the sea of white crosses memorializing those who died liberating the country. His family stands back, giving space to his memories. Five decades have passed since he was rescued and returned home. Five decades since the men gave their lives that he might live. Overcome by gratitude, Private James Ryan kneels before the tomb of Captain John Miller and breaks down in tears, like his mother on that porch so many years before.

Turning to his wife at last, he cries, "Tell me...tell me that I've lived a good life." She walks forward and wraps her arms around him as they weep together.

The tears come for me too, as I write. You see, I too have knelt before a cross. A cross that reminds me of the monumental sacrifice of the One who gave His life that I might live. And like Private Ryan, I feel a sense of unworthiness. Such love, such sacrifice, makes me want to *do* something. It seems to demand that I repay the Giver, that I sacrifice something in return. "Tell me," I want to say, "that I'm worthy, that I've lived up to this, that I've done enough, that I've run fast enough." Then comes the gentle reminder: "You haven't, Phil. There is nothing you can do to deserve this. Just accept it, it's all been done."

God's finished work in Christ Jesus has brought us salvation, redemption, reconciliation, resurrection, and eternity with Him. His death has brought us life. His grace has brought us Home. Nothing we do will ever make us worthy of such grace. Nothing we do will ever repay the debt. What can we do but accept the gift and live the rest of our lives with thanksgiving, reflecting that grace, mirroring for all around us the reality of the greatest reversal in all of history? God loves the unlovely, forgives the unforgivable, offers grace to the graceless, and provides a resting place to the busy and the burdened.

Like Dante, who at the end of his long ascent from hell to heaven heard a sound like the laughter of the universe, we celebrate the laughter of grace. "To laugh," writes Donald McCullough, "is to surrender, to capitulate to a surprising incongruity. Think of the stuff of which humor is made—a silly story about St. Peter at the Pearly Gates ends with an unexpected punch line; a preacher proceeds down the aisle gloriously oblivious to a strand of toilet paper caught in his belt and streaming behind like a vestment of embarrassment; a two-year-old decides a bowl would make a wonderful hat but doesn't bother to empty the spaghetti before putting it on her head; Charlie Chaplin slips on a banana peel—and we can't help but laugh. Laughter is a happy release of the tension created by an unexpected turn of events. And the grandest surprise of all, the greatest reversal ever, has happened by God's grace in Jesus Christ. Who could have guessed it? What can we do but surrender to it? Our response is like laughter..." Such surrender brings abundant joy. And abundant peace.

On the night of my thirty-fifth birthday, I tucked my eldest son into bed. I had already been contemplating my own mortality that day. And a trip to my son's room didn't help. "Dad," he said, looking up at me with a sideways glance, "how old are you again?"

"I'm 35, son," I answered.

"You're half-dead," whispered Stephen.

Tucking him calmly into bed, I went across the hallway and removed him from the will. Not really. But I remember sitting in the living room later, thinking, *I can't believe how fast 35 years of my life have gone! And we pick up speed the closer we get to home.*

If I'm getting this old, I thought to myself, *I'd better find out what I want on my tombstone.* So, in the ensuing days, I began looking. There are some pretty funny ones out there. There's one that says simply, "He should have ducked." Another says, "See, I told you I was sick." One of my favorites goes like this: "Here lies an atheist, all dressed up, no place to go."

I don't want anything funny on my tombstone. I simply want it to say this:

> He found God's grace
> too amazing
> to keep to himself.

In a fast-forward world such a mission brings freedom. We do not need to keep on running. Living at the speed of grace releases us to pause. To stop. To rest. To serve others out of love. To invest in the things that will outlive us. To live lives of thanksgiving. Passing God's grace along, all the way Home.

As an author, I am often asked about the writing process, and perhaps the best advice I've ever offered someone is, "Write on your knees." Before writing each of my books, I have spent time working out a simple prayer to God that reflects the theme and directs my heart. Many months ago, on the day this book began to take shape, I sat down and wrote out the following. Perhaps it is fitting to finish where this all began:

Heavenly Father,

Protect me from the distractions of a noisy culture,
that I may hear your voice—and listen.
Keep me from giving too much of my time to those
who won't cry at my funeral!
Grant me wisdom to separate the insignificant
from the eternal opportunities that intersect my path a hundred
times each day.
Restore my body with your rest, season my words with your
grace.

Free me from the sin of comparison, the trap of equating
popularity with value.
May the days I have left be lived at your pace,
as I greet the success of others with joy,
their pain with compassion, their failures with grace.
And in the end, may I be remembered by only a few
who saw You reflected in me.

Amen.

About the Author

Phil Callaway is an award-winning columnist and a popular speaker at conferences, churches, camps, Promise Keepers, and Focus on the Family. His greatest achievement was convincing his high school sweetheart to marry him. He has also taken out the garbage without being told twice. The author of a dozen books, including *Making Life Rich Without Any Money* and *Who Put the Skunk in the Trunk?: Learning to Laugh When Life Stinks!*, Phil's writings have been translated into such languages as Spanish, Polish, Indonesian, Chinese, and English—one of which he speaks fluently. His five-part video series, *The Big Picture,* has been circulated in thousands of churches worldwide. Phil and Ramona live in Alberta, Canada, with their three children.

For booking information, e-mail
vance.neudorf@pbi.ab.ca

For information on Phil's books, tapes, videos,
or speaking ministry, please call 403-443-5511,
check out his Web page at **www.philcallaway.ab.ca,**
or write him at:

PO Box 4576
Three Hills, Alberta T0M 2N0
CANADA

Phil is also editor of *Servant* magazine, an award-winning magazine read in 101 countries. A ministry of Prairie Bible Institute, *Servant* is full of insightful interviews with well-known Christians, helpful articles, world news, and Phil's trademark humor. For a complimentary one-year subscription, please call 1-800-221-8532, check out the Web page at **www.pbi.ab.ca/servant,** or write:

Servant Magazine
Box 4000
Three Hills, Alberta T0M 2N0
CANADA

Other Harvest House Reading

I USED TO HAVE ANSWERS, NOW I HAVE KIDS
by *Phil Callaway*

These sparkling, warmly told stories capture the amusing and bemusing experiences of life while sharing timeless spiritual lessons. Funny and inspiring, Phil reminds us that it's wonderful to be part of a family.

MAKING LIFE RICH WITHOUT ANY MONEY
by *Phil Callaway*

With humor and candor, award-winning storyteller Phil Callaway shows readers how to find the happiness of a millionaire on the salary of a servant. Truly wealthy people enjoy laughter, simplicity, forgiveness, and hope—whether they have money or not.

COFFEE CUP FRIENDSHIP AND CHEESECAKE FUN
by *Becky Freeman*

Becky's humorous insights encourage women to visit friends, laugh at life's quirks, and promote truth, love, friendship, and service. Along with delightful recipes and quotes, readers will discover that joy revolves around relationships and faith.

LEMONADE LAUGHTER AND LAID-BACK JOY
by *Becky Freeman*

Lemonade Laughter and Laid-Back Joy brings the surprising—and gratifying—news that Jesus Himself modeled a laid-back life. Through laugh-out-loud stories and encouraging insights, Becky guides readers to travel life on a less hurried, less worried path and embrace the gift that is today.

THE THINGS THAT MATTER MOST
by *Bob Welch*

In this collection of heartwarming stories you will find what is truly important: the people you cherish, the dreams you share, and the talents God has given exclusively to you.

A FATHER FOR ALL SEASONS
by *Bob Welch*

This highly personal book gives encouragement to dads and sons by reminding them that they need each other. Written by award-winning author Bob Welch, excerpts of this book have appeared in *Focus on the Family* and *Reader's Digest* magazines.